The Geography of Lo

Same-Sex Marriage &
Relationship Recognition
in America
(The Story in Maps)

Fifth Edition

Peter Nicolas & Mike Strong

Peter Nicolas
University of Washington School of Law
415 William H. Gates Hall
Box 353020
Seattle, Washington 98195-3020

pnicolas@uw.edu
www.gayrightsmap.com

ISBN-13: 978-1494838591
ISBN-10: 1494838591

****

The authors have created this publication to provide you with accurate and authoritative information concerning same-sex marriage and relationship recognition in the United States. However, this publication was not necessarily prepared by persons licensed to practice law in a particular jurisdiction. The authors are not engaged in rendering legal or other professional advice, and this publication is not a substitute for the advice of an attorney. If you require legal or other professional advice, you should seek the services of a licensed attorney or other professional in your jurisdiction.

Contents:

Map 1: **The status of same-sex marriage**

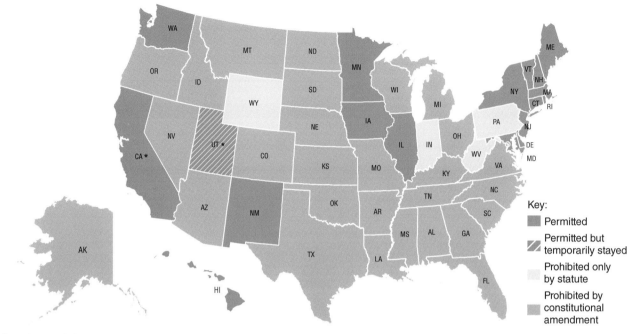

Key:

- Permitted
- Permitted but temporarily stayed
- Prohibited only by statute
- Prohibited by constitutional amendment

* State with a constitutional amendment prohibiting same-sex marriage that was struck down by a federal court.

Map 2: **Same-sex relationship recognition in the United States**

This map only includes states that allow same-sex couples to enter into legally recognized relationships within their borders. States that recognize same-sex relationships entered into in other states are detailed in Table 5.

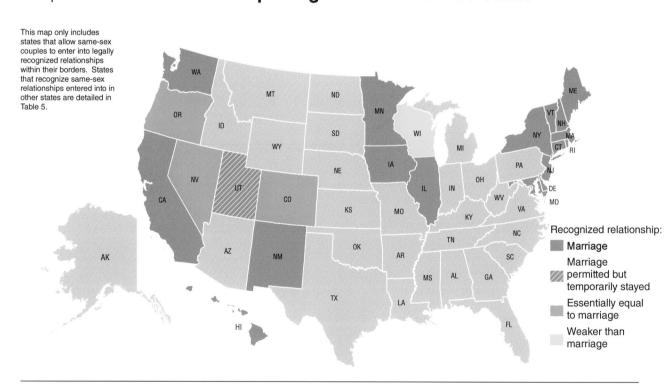

Recognized relationship:

- **Marriage**
- Marriage permitted but temporarily stayed
- Essentially equal to marriage
- Weaker than marriage

1

A brief history of legal recognition of same-sex relationships

Today, there is no question that the most prominent gay rights issue is the right to marry. With a few exceptions, the rights enjoyed by the vast majority of American couples are simply not available to same-sex couples in most parts of the United States.

When considering the question of same-sex marriage, it is impossible to look at it without considering domestic partnership and civil unions. These alternatives to marriage have given same-sex couples many if not all of the protections granted by states to married couples, and have been a precursor to marriage in several states.

This publication starts with a look at the legal recognition given to same-sex relationships across the country, followed by a look at the constitutional amendments against same-sex marriage enacted by various states. It concludes with an examination of important votes related to the recognition of same-sex relationships in selected states.

The 1970s & 1980s

The first[1] reported judicial challenge to state laws limiting marriage to opposite-sex couples was initiated after two men, Richard Baker and James McConnell, were denied a marriage license in Hennepin County, Minnesota on May 18, 1970.[2] Their constitutional challenge was rejected by the Minnesota state courts,[3] and an appeal to the U.S. Supreme Court was summarily dismissed on the ground that the case failed to raise a "substantial federal question."[4] Other constitutional challenges filed in the early 1970s in Kentucky[5] and Washington[6] also failed.[7]

These early challenges came at a high price for some of the litigants: not only did they lose their cases, they also lost or were denied public employment for bringing the high profile challenges, and those employment actions were upheld in separate judicial challenges.[8]

Same-sex couples brought a series of constitutional challenges to marriage laws in federal and state courts in California,[9] Ohio,[10] and Pennsylvania[11] in the early 1980s, but these were likewise rejected, with the courts citing

the earlier decisions from Minnesota, Washington, and Kentucky.[12]

For most of the remainder of the 1980s, the focus shifted away from the courts and toward local legislative bodies. Starting with the City of Berkeley, California in 1984 and the City of West Hollywood, California in 1985, respectively, local governments began to enact domestic partnership ordinances extending benefits to employees in same-sex relationships, as well as domestic partnership registries for members of the public-at-large.[13] While the latter was primarily of symbolic importance (largely, these registries provided same-sex couples with no legal rights), it was a step forward in that it was the first time that same-sex relationships received any form of official recognition. Other cities, including San Francisco and Seattle, enacted domestic partnership ordinances in the late 1980s.[14]

The end of the decade brought a glimmer of hope for legal recognition of same-sex relationships, as the New York Court of Appeals issued the first judicial decision recognizing in any way a relationship between two persons of the same sex. In that decision, the New York high court ruled that the word "family" as used in rent-control statutes referred not only to one's legal spouse, but also to one's unmarried same-sex life partner.[15]

The efforts by local governments to symbolically recognize same-sex relationships, and the limited success in the New York Court of Appeals, while welcome, did little to satisfy gay couples' desire for full relationship recognition, and thus the 1990s saw a series of additional judicial challenges to marriage laws.

The 1990s

The 1990s started off much the same way as the 1970s and 1980s, with New York[16] and District of Columbia[17] courts rejecting constitutional challenges to laws limiting marriage to persons of the opposite sex.

But in 1993, the Hawaii Supreme Court held that the equal protection guarantee of the Hawaii Constitution might (absent a sufficient justification by the state) invalidate the state's denial of marriage licenses to same-sex couples.[18] The Hawaii decision led to a panic in state legislatures and in Congress. Lawmakers feared that other states would be required to recognize same-sex marriages performed in Hawaii under the Full Faith and Credit Clause of the U.S. Constitution and its implementing statute, the Full Faith and Credit Act. Accordingly, in 1996, Congress enacted and President Clinton signed into law the Defense of Marriage Act (DOMA), which defined marriage for federal purposes as a union between one man and one woman, and amended the Full Faith and Credit Act to provide that states were not required to recognize same-sex marriages performed in other states.[19]

Although controversial, many supporters of gay rights argued that DOMA was a necessary evil, as it probably prevented an amendment to the U.S. Constitution that would have banned same-sex marriage altogether. That notwithstanding, DOMA complicated the lives of same-sex couples by preventing any sort of federal recognition of their relationships.

In the midst of the debates over DOMA, the U.S. Supreme Court, in *Romer v. Evans*,[20] struck down as unconstitutional, on federal equal protection grounds, a 1992 amendment to the Colorado Constitution that both repealed local ordinances banning discrimination on the basis of sexual orientation and prohibited all levels of state government from enacting any laws prohibiting discrimination on that basis. The decision marked the first time that the U.S. Supreme Court had invoked the equal protection clause—previously used to invalidate laws discriminating on the basis of race and gender—to strike down a law discriminating on the basis of sexual orientation.

Back in Hawaii, the legislature in 1997 (as part of an effort to respond to the 1993 decision) created a "reciprocal beneficiaries" registry that extended a very limited set of rights to unmarried couples who were legally prohibited from marrying.[21] That was followed in 1998 by a constitutional amendment at the ballot box in which voters overwhelmingly voted to give the legislature the exclusive power to define marriage, thus effectively nullifying the 1993 Hawaii Supreme Court decision. In that same election cycle, voters in Alaska approved a constitutional amendment defining marriage as the union of one man and one woman, a response to an Alaska court decision from earlier that year holding that the state's denial of marriage licenses to same-sex couples violated the Alaska Constitution.[22]

DOMA was thought to be insufficient by many conservatives (since DOMA did not prevent state courts from deciding to recognize out-of-state same-sex marriages or holding that same-sex couples have the right to marry under their state constitutions), and thus the battles moved to individual state legislatures and ballot boxes. The constitutional amendments in Alaska and Hawaii were the first of many in a battle that would play out over the next decade.

The 1990s ended with a significant advance in the rights of same-sex couples, when the Vermont Supreme Court held that the state constitution required the state to offer same-sex couples recognition of their relationships, either via marriage or something equivalent.[23] The state chose civil unions, which began in 2000.[24] The decision, while decided purely on state constitutional grounds, invoked and found persuasive the U.S. Supreme Court's 1996 decision in *Romer*.[25] About that same time, an appeals court in Oregon, while not addressing the right to marry *per se*, held that a state university had an obligation under the Oregon constitution to extend to same-sex couples the same benefits that it gave to married opposite-sex couples.[26] In addition, in 1999, the California Legislature enacted the first statewide domestic partnership registry, which granted a limited set of rights to same-sex couples.[27]

2000 to 2002

The first decade of the second millennium brought more developments in the fight for marriage. Both sides in the fight experienced advancement and disappointment.

At the beginning of the decade, voters in California approved a law limiting marriage to opposite-sex couples.[28] Later in the year, a constitutional prohibition was enacted by voters in Nebraska, which ultimately was followed by more than two dozen other states over the next ten years. In most cases, the bans attracted widespread support, polling well over 50 percent at the ballot box in almost every state.

In 2001, the California Legislature expanded its domestic partnership law by adding additional rights.[29]

In 2002, a small bipartisan group of members of Congress introduced a proposal to amend the U.S. Constitution to define marriage as the union of one man and one woman and to further provide that neither the United States Constitution nor the constitution of any state be construed to extend either the right to marry or the benefits thereof to other unions, such as those between two individuals of the same-sex. The bill failed to advance to a vote in either chamber of Congress.

2003 & 2004

While the forces of prohibition seemed to have the upper-hand at the start of the millennium, two court decisions and the actions of a legislature substantially advanced gay rights generally and the right to marry specifically. First, in June 2003, the U.S. Supreme Court, in *Lawrence v. Texas*,[30] overruled its 1986 decision in *Bowers v. Hardwick*[31] and held that laws criminalizing sodomy violate the due process clause of the U.S. Constitution. In a strongly worded dissent, Justice Scalia warned that the decision cast doubt on the constitutionality of bans on same-sex marriage.[32]

Just a few months later, Justice Scalia's prediction came true. In November 2003, the Massachusetts high court surprised the country by holding that the equal protection and due process provisions of the state's constitution required that the right to marry be extended to same-sex couples.[33] Unlike its sister court in Vermont, the Massachusetts high court subsequently ruled that a substitute for same-sex couples, such as civil unions, was likewise unconstitutional.[34] Although the Massachusetts high court relied solely on the provisions of the Massachusetts Constitution, it cited as persuasive both the U.S. Supreme Court's 1996 decision in *Romer* as well as the Court's recent decision in *Lawrence*.[35]

The Massachusetts decision was stayed by the court for 6 months to give the legislature time to implement the decision,[36] and by the middle of 2004, Massachusetts became the first state in the nation to lawfully permit same-sex couples to wed. There were several efforts made to amend the Massachusetts Constitution, but because of the difficult process required to amend it, the question whether to amend the constitution never appeared before Massachusetts voters.

While all of that activity was taking place in the courts, state and local lawmakers were also taking steps to advance relationship recognition for same-sex couples. First, in September 2003, the California Legislature expanded its domestic partnership law, effective January 1, 2005, to include all of the rights associated with marriage.[37] Next, in January, 2004, the New Jersey Legislature enacted a domestic partnership law that granted same-sex couples a limited set of rights.[38] Then, in February 2004, before the changes in Massachusetts actually went into effect, Mayor Gavin Newsom of San Francisco—relying in part on the decision by the Massachusetts high court—concluded that denying same-sex couples the right to marry was unconstitutional, and thus ordered the city clerk to begin issuing marriage licenses to same-sex couples.[39] This led to a rush of marriages performed in the city, which dominated talk shows for a time. Mayor Newsom's actions were repeated by local leaders in various other jurisdictions, including Multnomah County, Oregon[40] and New Paltz, New York.[41] Eventually, the marriage licenses issued in these jurisdictions were invalidated by courts on the ground that the officials lacked the authority to issue them.[42] Finally, in April 2004, Maine's legislature created a statewide domestic partnership registry that extended a limited set of rights to same-sex and other unmarried couples.[43]

The events in Massachusetts, California and elsewhere gave the movement to ban same-sex marriage renewed energy. A proposal to amend the U.S. Constitution both to define marriage as the union of a man and a woman and to further provide that neither the U.S. Constitution nor that of any state be construed to require that marriage or the benefits thereof be extended to same-sex couples was reintroduced in Congress, and received the strong support of President George W. Bush. The proposal advanced to a debate in the full House and Senate in 2004, but failed to overcome a filibuster in the Senate and in the House received less than the two-thirds support required for constitutional amendments.

Although the proposed amendment to the U.S. Constitution failed, later that year, voters in 13 states from Arkansas to Utah approved amendments to their state constitutions. While the percentages of people voting yes varied, the results were the same, with voters deciding to ban same-sex marriage, and in some cases, other forms of relationship recognition as well.

2005 to 2007

The year 2005 brought more constitutional amendments in Kansas and Texas, but also a civil union law in Connecticut, which was signed into law by a Republican governor following the initiation of a lawsuit challenging the state's denial of marriage licenses to same-sex couples.[44] In 2005 (and again in 2007), the California Legislature voted to extend the right to marry to same-sex couples, but the bills were vetoed by the governor.[45]

Three separate state high courts weighed in on the issue of same-sex marriage in 2006. The high courts in both New York and Washington rejected claims that their state constitutions required that the right to marry be extended to same-sex couples.[46] Early in 2006, the New Jersey

Legislature modestly expanded the rights included in the state's domestic partnership program.[47] Later that year, the New Jersey high court ruled that although the state's constitution did not necessarily require that same-sex couples be given the right to marry, its equal protection guarantee required that they be given the same rights and privileges of marriage.[48] As a result, the state legislature enacted a civil union law that provided same-sex couples with all of the rights associated with marriage.[49]

Autumn 2006 led to the next and last large wave of anti-same-sex marriage constitutional amendments. With the exception of Arizona, all the amendments passed. Arizona voters surprised conservatives by narrowly rejecting an amendment that would ban same-sex marriage as well as other forms of relationship recognition, such as civil unions. This was the first and only time an amendment banning same-sex marriage failed at the ballot box. (A revised law banning only same-sex marriage passed two years later by a healthy margin.)

In 2007, Maryland's high court held that neither the due process and equal protection provisions of the Maryland Constitution nor its Equal Rights Amendment required extension of the right to marry to same-sex couples.[50] That same year, the New Hampshire Legislature voted to create civil unions for same-sex couples starting on January 1 of the following year,[51] becoming the first state to do so without either a court order or pending litigation.[52] In addition, in Washington, the legislature voted to create a statewide domestic partnership registry that extended a limited set of rights to same-sex couples.[53] Lastly, the Oregon Legislature enacted a domestic partnership law that extended all the rights of marriage to same-sex couples to take effect on January 1 of the following year.[54]

2008

Early in 2008, the Washington Legislature voted to significantly expand the number of rights for those registered as state domestic partners.[55] Then, in May of that year, the Supreme Court of California caused a political earthquake by interpreting the state constitution's equal protection, due process, and privacy clauses to require extending the right to marry to same-sex couples.[56]

This set off not only a rush of same-sex weddings, but also a rush by conservatives to collect signatures for a constitutional amendment defining marriage as between one man and one woman. Ultimately, they gathered the required number of signatures and the amendment (known as "Proposition 8") was approved at the ballot

box by a margin of 52 percent in favor to 48 percent opposed.

This stopped any further same-sex couples from marrying in the state, but the Supreme Court of California—while rejecting a challenge to the method in which the California Constitution was amended—upheld the validity of the marriages performed before the election.[57]

Just days before California voters approved Proposition 8, the Supreme Court of Connecticut held that the equal protection provision of the state's constitution required that the right to marry be extended to same-sex couples, rejecting an argument that the "separate" but "equal" institution of civil unions for same-sex couples was sufficient to satisfy equal protection guarantees.[58] Days later, Connecticut voters rejected a proposal (which appears on the ballot automatically every twenty years)[59] asking whether to convene a constitutional convention to amend or revise the constitution (at which the newly announced state constitutional right to same-sex marriage could have been overturned) by a margin of 59 percent to 41 percent. Months later, the legislature voted to amend its marriage laws to mirror the court's decision.[60]

In 2008, Maryland's Legislature enacted a very modest law creating a statewide definition of a "domestic partner" and granting those who meet the definition hospital visitation and medical decisionmaking rights, the right to control the disposition of one another's remains, and exemption from the state's inheritance tax.[61] The Maryland law did not create a statewide registry, however, and those seeking to invoke the rights set forth in the law have to prove they meet the legal definition of "domestic partner."

2009

Proposition 8 was unquestionably a blow to advocates of same-sex marriage, but 2009 brought some dramatic advances, as well as more disappointments. Legislatures in Vermont and New Hampshire—which had previously offered same-sex couples only civil unions—voted to extend the right to marry to same-sex couples.[62] The Supreme Court of Iowa unanimously held that the equal protection clause of the Iowa Constitution required that the right to marry be extended to same-sex couples,[63] becoming the first state in the midwest to legalize same-sex marriage. Progressive legislators in Iowa managed to block efforts to overturn the decision by an amendment to the state's constitution.

Maine's legislature also voted to extend the right to marry to same-sex couples, but the law was overturned by voters before it could go into effect via Question 1, which succeeded by a margin of 53 to 47 percent in the November 2009 election.

In Washington State, the legislature expanded its existing domestic partnership program to include all the rights associated with marriage.[64] Citizen activists gathered enough signatures to put the issue of expansion on the November 2009 ballot. In the election, voters—by a margin of 53 to 47 percent—upheld the expansion of the domestic partnership program, the first time any state electorate had voted to affirm same-sex partnerships.

Legislative action took place in several other states as well. In Nevada, the legislature enacted a domestic partnership law that extended the rights of marriage to same-sex couples.[65] In Colorado, the legislature enacted a modest designated beneficiary agreement law, designed to make it easier for same-sex and other unmarried couples to obtain certain limited rights.[66] And in Wisconsin, the legislature enacted a domestic partnership law that extended a limited set of rights to same-sex couples.[67] In December 2009, the New York Senate disappointed many by rejecting a measure to extend the right to marry to same-sex couples (many of the votes against the bill were cast by Democrats from the outer boroughs of New York City).

2010

In March 2010, the District of Columbia became the sixth jurisdiction in the United States to extend the right to marry to same-sex couples after a law enacted by the city council and signed by the mayor went into effect without a veto by Congress.[68] In April 2010, the Hawaii legislature voted to create civil unions for same-sex couples, but the legislation was vetoed by Hawaii's governor.

In the latter half of 2010, federal district courts on opposite sides of the country issued decisions with the potential to reshape the future of marriage rights for same-sex couples in the United States. First, a federal district court in Massachusetts—one of the few states at the time in which same-sex couples were permitted to marry—invoked both the equal protection guarantee of the U.S. Constitution and the Tenth Amendment (which reserves to the states powers not given by the Constitution to the federal government) to strike down that portion of DOMA that defines marriage for federal purposes as a union between one man and one woman, thus requiring the federal government to extend the federal rights

associated with marriage to same-sex couples.[69] That was followed by a decision by a federal district court in California holding that California's Proposition 8 violates the equal protection and due process guarantees of the U.S. Constitution.[70]

Although the November 2010 election did not have any initiatives on the ballot regarding same-sex marriage or relationship recognition, voters in Iowa did indirectly send a message regarding the Iowa Supreme Court's 2009 decision. Pursuant to state law, three of the seven justices on the Iowa Supreme Court were up for a retention vote, and by a margin of about 54 to 46 percent, voters chose not to retain those justices on the Court, temporarily reducing its size to just four justices. Shortly after the retention election, conservative legislators in Iowa started to advocate in favor of impeachment proceedings for the remaining four justices.

2011

In 2011, advocates for same-sex marriage and relationship recognition scored major legislative victories in several states, made progress in others, and received support for their efforts to challenge DOMA in the courts from the Obama Administration. And while opponents of same-sex marriage persuaded legislators in two states to place constitutional amendments banning same-sex marriage before voters, advocates of same-sex marriage managed to block serious efforts to do so in several other states.

The year started off with legislative victories for advocates of same-sex relationship recognition in Illinois and Hawaii. In January and February, respectively, the governors of those states signed bills creating civil union programs that provide same-sex as well as opposite-sex couples all of the rights and responsibilities associated with marriage, with the Illinois program going into effect on June 1, 2011 and the Hawaii program going into effect on January 1, 2012.[71]

These legislative victories were followed by two major legislative disappointments, with legislatures in Maryland and Rhode Island narrowly defeating efforts to legalize same-sex marriage in those states despite strong political support from both their governors and significant numbers of their state legislators.

In turn, these political setbacks were followed by major successes on both the legislative and judicial fronts in Delaware, New York, Rhode Island, and Wyoming. In May, Delaware's governor signed a bill creating a civil union program that provides same-sex couples all of the rights and responsibilities associated with marriage, which took effect on January 1, 2012.[72] In June, the Wyoming Supreme Court held that, under Wyoming law, out-of-state same-sex marriages will be recognized, at least for purposes of granting a divorce.[73] That same month, New York's governor signed a bill legalizing same-sex marriage, making it the sixth state (along with the District of Columbia) to permit same-sex couples to marry.[74] Finally, as a compromise following failed efforts to legalize same-sex marriage, the Rhode Island legislature enacted—and in July its governor signed—a bill creating a civil union program providing same-sex couples all of the rights and responsibilities associated with marriage that took effect immediately.[75]

In the midst of all of these successes, U.S. Attorney General Eric Holder announced in February that the Obama Administration had concluded that Section 3 of DOMA—which defines marriage for purposes of federal law as the union between one man and one woman and denies federal benefits to same-sex couples married in states that permit them to marry—is unconstitutional and declined to defend its constitutionality in several court challenges filed by same-sex couples in federal district courts located in the northeast. Following that announcement, the U.S. House of Representatives voted to hire outside counsel to defend the law on behalf of Congress.

Moreover, following the official repeal of the military's Don't Ask, Don't Tell policy in September, the Pentagon announced that military chaplains could perform same-sex marriages in any state where such marriages are not prohibited by state law.

In the meantime, opponents of same-sex marriage made a serious legislative push to place constitutional amendments banning same-sex marriage before voters in Minnesota, North Carolina, and Wyoming. Legislators in North Carolina voted to place the question before voters in the May 2012 primary, while those in Minnesota voted to place the question before voters in the November 2012 general election. However, the Wyoming Senate blocked efforts to place a constitutional amendment before voters.

As 2011 drew to a close, serious efforts were underway to take the right to marry away from same-sex couples in Iowa and New Hampshire. In New Hampshire, Republicans gained a veto-proof majority in the legislature in the 2010 election, and moved forward with plans to repeal marriage rights for same-sex couples and replace them with civil unions. In Iowa, efforts to begin the process of placing

a constitutional amendment before voters that would ban same-sex marriage and other forms of relationship recognition were narrowly thwarted in the Iowa Senate.

2012 & 2013

The years 2012 and 2013 are certain to go down in the history books as game-changing years in the legal and political battle to advance marriage rights for same-sex couples.

The first three months of 2012 witnessed a flurry of legislative activity, with legislatures in New Jersey, Maryland, and Washington sending bills legalizing same-sex marriage to their respective governors. While New Jersey's governor vetoed the bill, the governors of Maryland and Washington signed them.[76] At the same time, New Hampshire's Republican-controlled legislature rejected a bill to repeal marriage rights for same-sex couples and replace them with civil unions by a resounding margin of 211-116. In addition, supporters of same-sex marriage in Maine collecting enough signatures to place a proposal on the November 2012 ballot that, if approved by voters, would extend marriage rights to same-sex couples. While all of this was occurring, the U.S. Court of Appeals for the Ninth Circuit held that California's Proposition 8 violated the equal protection guarantee of the U.S. Constitution.[77]

Advocates of same-sex marriage experienced a number of setbacks in the next three months, with voters in North Carolina approving a constitutional amendment prohibiting not only same-sex marriage, but all other types of legal unions as well, by a margin of 61 to 39 percent. Moreover, opponents of same-sex marriage in Maryland and Washington collected enough signatures to place their states' new marriage equality laws on hold and to force a public vote on the measures in the November 2012 general election.

During this period, the U.S. Court of Appeals for the First Circuit struck down on equal protection grounds that portion of DOMA that defines marriage for federal purposes as a union between one man and one woman, becoming the first federal appeals court to do so.[78] It was joined several months later by the U.S. Court of Appeals for the Second Circuit.[79]

As the November 2012 general election drew near, polls showed all four states where marriage was before voters—Maine, Maryland, Minnesota, and Washington—as too close to call, and advocates of same-sex marriage were hopeful that they might win one or more of these contests. Yet on election day, the results were better than any of them could have imagined, with voters in Minnesota rejecting the constitutional amendment banning same-sex marriage while voters in Maine, Maryland, and Washington all approved extending the right to marry to same-sex couples. Moreover, voters in Iowa not only voted to retain one of the Iowa Supreme Court Justices who voted to strike down the state's ban on same-sex marriage, but gave supporters of same-sex marriage control of the Iowa Senate, making a constitutional amendment in that state unlikely in the foreseeable future.

As 2012 drew to a close, the U.S. Supreme Court decided to review the Ninth Circuit's decision striking down California's Proposition 8, and to review the Second Circuit's decision striking down that portion of DOMA defining marriage as the union between one man and one woman for federal purposes.[80]

With the November 2012 elections demonstrating that support for same-sex marriage was no longer a losing issue with voters, advocates of same-sex marriage and relationship recognition experienced numerous legislative successes during the first half of 2013. In March, Colorado enacted a statewide civil union program that provides same-sex as well as opposite-sex couples with all of the rights and responsibilities associated with marriage, which took effect on May 1.[81] In May, Delaware,[82] Minnesota,[83] and Rhode Island[84] legalized same-sex marriage, with the Delaware law taking effect on July 1 and the Minnesota and Rhode Island laws taking effect on August 1. In addition, in May, the Nevada legislature took the first step in the process of repealing the state's constitutional amendment banning same-sex marriage.

These legislative victories were followed in June by two major victories in the United States Supreme Court. First, in *Hollingsworth v. Perry*,[85] the Supreme Court held that the supporters of California's Proposition 8 lacked standing to seek review of the 2010 federal district court decision declaring Proposition 8 to be unconstitutional, the effect of which was that same-sex marriages resumed in California almost immediately. Second, in *United States v. Windsor*,[86] the Supreme Court declared that portion of DOMA defining marriage as the union between one man and one woman for federal purposes to be unconstitutional, the effect of which was federal recognition of same-sex marriages entered into in states where same-sex marriage is permitted. In a strongly worded dissenting opinion in *Windsor*, Justice Scalia warned that the logic of the

Court's decision would inevitably result in state laws that refuse to recognize same-sex marriages lawfully entered into in other states—as well as state laws prohibiting same-sex couples from marrying—being struck down as unconstitutional.[87]

An open question after *Windsor* is whether federal recognition of same-sex marriages is tied to the legality of same-sex marriage in the state in which the couple *entered* into the marriage, or the legality of same-sex marriage in the state in which the couple is *domiciled* when they seek federal recognition. As this book goes to press, there remains uncertainty on that issue, and it currently varies depending upon the federal benefit sought (because the statutes creating those benefits use somewhat different wording). Thus, for example, for joint federal income tax filing and immigration rights, the marriage will be recognized so long as it was entered into in a state where same-sex marriage was lawful, even if the couple is domiciled in a state that does not recognize same-sex marriage.[88] In contrast, social security benefits are currently available only if the marriage is recognized as lawful in the state in which the couple is domiciled when benefits are sought; if it is not—even if it was lawful in the jurisdiction it was entered into—requests for benefits are neither granted nor rejected, but are currently put on "hold" pending further guidance.[89]

The Supreme Court's twin decisions in *Hollingsworth* and *Windsor* meant that same-sex couples could now marry in 13 states plus the District of Columbia and have their relationships recognized in most instances by the federal government. In the second half of 2013, those decisions were followed by a series of legislative and judicial victories that would significantly increase the number of states where same-sex couples could marry.

One month after the Supreme Court's decisions, a clerk in Montgomery County, Pennsylvania began issuing marriage licenses to same-sex couples based on his conclusion that the state's law banning same-sex marriage was unconstitutional in the wake of *Windsor*, but a court ordered him to stop doing so on September 12, 2013.[90] The status of the marriages entered into as a result of the clerk's actions—as well as the constitutionality of Pennsylvania's ban on same-sex marriage—are being litigated as this book goes to press.

In September, a state trial court in New Jersey declared that the state's law prohibiting same-sex marriage violated the equal protection guarantee of the state's constitution.[91] After the New Jersey Supreme Court rejected the state's motion for a stay pending an appeal of the decision,[92]

New Jersey's governor decided to drop the state's appeal, and same-sex marriages began in that state in October.[93]

In November, the governors of Hawaii and Illinois signed bills legalizing same-sex marriage into law, with the Hawaii law taking effect in December 2013[94] and the Illinois law taking effect in June 2014[95] (federal court orders issued in December 2013, however, require that couples in which one partner has a life-threatening illness be allowed to marry in Illinois prior to the effective date).[96]

In December, the New Mexico Supreme Court unanimously held that the state's prohibition on same-sex marriage violated the equal protection guarantee of the state's constitution.[97] The decision was preceded in August by a clerk in Doña Ana County issuing marriage licenses on his own initiative as well as a series of lower court decisions declaring the state's prohibition unconstitutional.[98]

In the final days of 2013, federal judges in Ohio and Utah cited Justice Scalia's warning in his dissent in *Windsor* in support of their decisions to strike down laws regarding same-sex marriage in those states.[99] The Ohio decision—while not addressing the question whether Ohio must permit same-sex couples to marry—held that under the Equal Protection and Due Process Clauses of the U.S. Constitution, Ohio was required to recognize same-sex marriages entered into in other states, at least in certain circumstances.[100] In contrast, the Utah decision held that under those same two constitutional provisions, not only did the state have to recognize out-of-state same-sex marriages, but also that it had to let same-sex couples marry within the state.[101] The Utah decision took effect while an appeal of the decision was pending, allowing over 1,000 same-sex couples in Utah to obtain marriage licenses (and many of those to marry) before the United States Supreme Court intervened and stayed the decision pending the state's appeal to the U.S. Court of Appeals for the Tenth Circuit[102] (The Tenth Circuit itself had previously declined to issue a stay on the ground that the state was unlikely to win the appeal). Because the Tenth Circuit, in denying the stay, indicated that the state was unlikely to win its appeal, this book assumes that same-sex marriages will eventually resume in Utah, and treats Utah as a state where same-sex couples can marry in all maps, tables, and figures that follow.

The Future

A string of legislative and judicial victories over the past decade have brought same-sex marriage and relationship recognition to nearly all regions of the United States except for the South. Until recently, constitutional amendments banning same-sex marriage enshrined into state constitutions in a majority of states have limited the ability of advocates of same-sex marriage to significantly expand marriage rights outside of states in the northeast and western United States. However, the U.S. Supreme Court's 2013 decision in *Windsor* has provided support for efforts by advocates of same-sex marriage to invoke successfully the U.S. Constitution as a basis for challenging the constitutionality of state laws banning same-sex marriage. As this book goes to press, lawsuits challenging such amendments are pending in nearly every state that still prohibits same-sex marriage.

Even as those decisions work their way through the courts, couples in states where same-sex marriage is prohibited can nonetheless obtain some rights by getting married in a state where same-sex marriage is permitted. Although at this time such marriages will not be recognized by their home state, the federal government's reaction to the *Windsor* decision means that such couples will be able to obtain at least partial federal recognition of their marriage and the benefits that follow from such recognition.

2 Existing recognition of same-sex relationships

Marriage

As indicated in Section 1, eighteen states and the District of Columbia allow same-sex couples to marry. Massachusetts, in 2004, became the first state where same-sex couples could legally wed, followed by California, Connecticut, Iowa, Vermont, New Hampshire, the District of Columbia, New York, Washington, Maine, Maryland, Delaware, Minnesota, Rhode Island, New Jersey, Hawaii, Illinois, New Mexico and Utah. (In California, same-sex marriages occured for a few months in 2008, were halted as a result of a state constitutional amendment, and resumed in 2013 when litigation over the amendment's constitutionality was completed. In Utah, same-sex marriages occurred for a few weeks in 2013 and 2014 but were halted by the United States Supreme Court pending the conclusion of appellate review.) In these nineteen jurisdictions, same-sex marriage is treated identically to opposite-sex marriage by state and local government for all purposes.[103]

Figure 1 shows the percentage of the U.S. population living in states that permit same-sex couples to marry. Table 1 compares the states that permit same-sex

Table 1: States that allow same-sex couples to marry

Jurisdiction	Year Effective	Civil Unions or Domestic Partnerships First?	Path to Legalization
California	2008[104]	Yes	California Supreme Court, Federal District Court
Connecticut	2008	Yes, as a response to a lawsuit	Connecticut Supreme Court
Delaware	2013	Yes	State legislature
Hawaii	2013	Yes	State legislature
Illinois	2014[105]	Yes	State legislature
Iowa	2009	No	Iowa Supreme Court
Maine	2012	Yes	Citizen-initiated public vote
Maryland	2013[106]	No[107]	State legislature, ratified by public vote
Massachusetts	2004[108]	No	Massachusetts Supreme Judicial Court
Minnesota	2013	No	State legislature
New Hampshire	2010[109]	Yes	State legislature
New Jersey	2013	Yes, due to court order	State Superior Court
New Mexico	2013	No	New Mexico Supreme Court
New York	2011	No	State legislature
Rhode Island	2013	Yes	State legislature
Utah	2013	No	Federal District Court (stayed pending appeal)
Vermont	2009	Yes, due to court order	State legislature
Washington	2012	Yes	State legislature, ratified by public vote
Washington, D.C.	2010[109]	Yes	City Council

Table 2: How can couples marry?

Jurisdiction	Fee[110]	Residency Required?	Blood Test ?	Minimum Age	Waiting Period	Procedure
California	Varies	No	No	18[111]	No	Both must apply for license in person.[112] Ceremony must occur within 90 days of license issuance.
Connecticut	$30	No	No	18[113]	No	Both must apply for license in person. Must have ceremony within 65 days after date of application.
Delaware	$50[114]	No	No	18[115]	24 hours	Both must apply for license in person.[116] Ceremony must occur within 30 days of license issuance.
Hawaii	$65	No	No	18[117]	No	Both must apply for license in person. Ceremony must occur within 30 days of license issuance.
Illinois	Varies	No[118]	No	18[119]	1 day	Both must apply for license in person. Ceremony must occur within 60 days of license issuance.
Iowa	$35	No	No	18[120]	3 days[121]	May apply for license in person or by mail. The license must be picked up in person within 6 months of the application date.
Maine	$40	No	No	18[122]	No	Must file notice of intentions to marry by mail or in person, but both must appear in person to obtain marriage license. Ceremony must occur within 90 days of filing notice of intentions to marry.
Maryland	Varies	No	No	18[123]	2 days[124]	At least one party must apply for license in person. Ceremony must occur within 6 months of date license becomes effective.
Massachusetts	Varies	No	No	18[125]	3 days[126]	Both must file notice of intent to marry and take oath in person.[127] Ceremony must occur within 60 days of filing notice.
Minnesota	$115[128]	No	No	18[129]	5 days[130]	At least one party must apply for license in person. Ceremony must occur within 6 months of license issuance.
New Hampshire	$45	No[131]	No	18[132]	No	Both must fill out application for marriage license in person.[133] Ceremony must occur within 90 days of application.
New Jersey	$28	No	No	18[134]	72 hours[135]	Both must apply for license in person.[136] Ceremony must occur within 30 days of license issuance.
New Mexico	$25	No	No	18[137]	No	Both must apply for license in person.[138]
New York	$35-40[139]	No	Yes[140]	18[141]	24 hours[142]	Both must apply for license in person. Ceremony must occur within 60 days of license issuance.[143]
Rhode Island	$24	No	No	18[144]	No	Both must apply for license in person. Ceremony must occur within 3 months of license issuance.
Utah#	Varies	No	No	18[145]	No	Both must apply for license in person. Ceremony must occur within 30 days of license issuance.
Vermont	$45	No	No	18[146]	No	At least one party must apply for the license in person. Ceremony must occur within 60 days of license issuance.
Washington	Varies	No	No	18[147]	3 days	Some counties permit application by mail, while others require applicants to appear in person. Ceremony must occur within 60 days of license issuance.
Washington, D.C.	$35	No	No	18[148]	3 days[149]	Both must apply in person and take an oath.

#Same-sex marriages have been suspended pending appellate court review of federal court decision striking down the state's ban on same-sex marriages.

couples to marry on three different axes: the year in which same-sex marriages began; the path to legalization; and whether same-sex marriage was preceded by statewide civil unions or domestic partnerships.

Table 2 provides detailed information about the prerequisites for getting married in each of these nineteen jurisdictions, including: the marriage license

Figure 1: Population in states where same-sex marriage is performed

Number of states:	18 plus the District of Columbia
Population:	121,230,843
% US population:	39.3%

Source: 2010 Census. Totals include Utah.

fee; minimum age and blood test requirements; whether non-residents are permitted to marry; and the waiting period, if any, between applying for a license and getting married.

With the exceptions of Illinois and New Hampshire, out-of-state couples are free to get married in these states, even if such marriages are banned in their home states (under Illinois and New Hampshire law, out-of-state couples cannot enter into marriages that are deemed "void" under the law of their home states). But those planning a weekend trip to one of these states to get married may be disappointed, as many of them require an in-person application followed by a waiting period of up to 5 days before the ceremony itself can occur.

Statewide Civil Unions and Domestic Partnerships

Four states that do not permit same-sex couples to marry nonetheless allow them to receive formal recognition of their relationships to some degree through domestic partnerships or civil unions. The legal protections afforded by these programs vary, with some providing same-sex couples with only a handful of rights and others

providing all of the rights associated with marriage. Table 3 compares the four states that only permit same sex couples to enter into civil unions or domestic partnerships across three different axes: the name of the program; the year it was first enacted (and subsequently amended); and whether it is essentially equivalent to marriage or instead provides only a limited set of rights and responsibilities.

In some instances, recognition of same-sex couples through these alternative programs is a step toward extending the right to marry to same-sex couples. Thus, twelve jurisdictions that currently recognize same-sex marriage—California, Connecticut, Delaware, Hawaii, Illinois, Maine, New Hampshire, New Jersey, Rhode Island, Vermont, Washington and the District of Columbia—previously allowed same-sex couples to

Figure 2: Population in states where same-sex marriage or other unions are performed

Number of states:	22 plus the District of Columbia
Population:	138,478,650
% US population:	44.9%

Source: 2010 Census. Totals include Utah.

enter into civil unions or domestic partnerships (under Connecticut, Delaware, New Hampshire and Washington law, those civil unions or domestic partnerships will automatically convert into marriages, while in California, Hawaii, Illinois, Maine, New Jersey, Rhode Island, Vermont and the District of Columbia, they will remain civil unions or domestic partnerships unless the couple affirmatively decides to marry).

In some states, these programs are available only to same-sex couples, while in other states, they are open to all couples. In some states, as with marriage, couples register with a county or municipal agency, while in other states, they register with a state agency, such as the Secretary of State.

Table 3: Overview of non-marital relationship recognition programs

State	Name of Program	Year Enacted	Subsequently Amended	Equal to Marriage?
Colorado	Civil Union	2009[150]	2013	Yes
Nevada	Domestic Partnership	2009		Yes[151]
Oregon	Domestic Partnership	2007[152]		Yes
Wisconsin	Domestic Partnership	2009		No

Table 4 compares the method of creating and dissolving the relationships in these states across seven different axes: agency with whom the couple registers; cost of registration; whether eligibility is limited to same-sex couples; whether a formal solemnization ceremony before a public or religious official is required; whether a waiting period is required; proof of relationship; and method of termination.

Some of the states that offer these alternatives to marriage have constitutional amendments defining marriage as the union of one man and one woman. One state—Wisconsin—also has a constitutional amendment banning civil unions and domestic partnerships that are identical or substantially similar to marriage, and a challenge to the validity of Wisconsin's domestic partnership law is currently pending before the Wisconsin Supreme Court.

To date, the term "civil union" has always referred to a program that provides all of the rights and responsibilities associated with marriage. In contrast, the term "domestic partnership" is associated with a range of programs: the domestic partnership programs in Nevada and Oregon provide all of the rights and responsibilities associated with marriage, while that in Wisconsin provides a more limited basket of rights.

Of the 23 jurisdictions that permit same-sex couples to either marry or enter into civil unions or domestic partnerships, all but one—Wisconsin—provide same-sex couples with all of the rights and responsibilities associated with marriage. These include such key rights as the testimonial privilege (the right not to testify against one another in court); the right to sue for the wrongful death of the spouse or partner; the right to inherit a designated share of the spouse or partner's estate if they die without a will; the right to control the disposition of the spouse or partner's remains; and the right to seek court-ordered spousal support upon dissolution of the relationship. Yet even Wisconsin provides all of these key rights, save for spousal support.

Figure 2 shows the percentage of the U.S. population living in states that permit same-sex couples to either marry or enter into civil unions, or domestic partnerships.

Recognition of Out-of-State Same-Sex Relationships Formalized in Other States

For opposite-sex couples, moving or traveling from one state or country to another typically has no impact on their legal status: the general, long-standing rule of law throughout the nation has been that a marriage that is valid in the state or country that it was entered into will be recognized as valid in other states.

States, however, have always maintained the authority to refuse to recognize out-of-state marriages to the extent that they violate a strong public policy of the state. Thus, for example, virtually no state will recognize an incestuous or polygamous marriage, even if it was lawfully entered into in another state or country.

Table 4: Formation and termination of non-marital relationship recognition programs

State	Register With	Cost	Eligibility	Ceremony Required	Waiting Period	Proof of Relationship	Method of Termination
Colorado	County Clerk	$30	Same or opposite sex	Yes[153]	No	Certificate of civil union	Dissolution or invalidation (annulment)
Nevada	Secretary of State	$50	Same or opposite sex	No	No	Certificate of registered domestic partnership	Dissolution (simplified procedure for those with no children, registered fewer than 5 years, and other criteria)
Oregon	County Clerk	Varies	Same sex	No	No	Certificate of registered domestic partnership	Dissolution or annulment
Wisconsin	County Clerk	Varies	Same sex	No	No	Certified copy of declaration of domestic partnership	Unilateral termination with service or notice; mutual termination; marriage of either party

As detailed in Section 3, as state courts started to hold that same-sex couples had a right to marry, dozens of states nationwide enacted statutes or constitutional amendments defining marriage as the union of one man and one woman and expressly providing that they would refuse to recognize same-sex marriages entered into in other states (some of these laws go further, refusing to recognize not only same-sex marriages, but also their functional equivalent, such as civil unions or domestic partnerships). In addition, the federal government enacted DOMA, which purports to give states the right not to recognize same-sex marriages lawfully entered into in other states.

Nonetheless, two categories of states recognize out-of-state same-sex marriages, civil unions, and domestic partnerships. The first category of states are those that themselves permit same-sex couples to enter into same-sex marriages, civil unions, or domestic partnerships. In the second category are states that do not themselves allow same-sex couples to enter into such relationships, but will recognize such relationships if validly entered into in another state.

Table 5 provides details on out-of-state recognition by the nineteen jurisdictions that currently permit same-sex couples to marry as well as the four states that only permit same-sex couples to enter into domestic partnerships or civil unions. In addition, it lists three other states—Arizona, Ohio and Wyoming—that have legal authority holding that they will recognize such relationships when validly entered into in another state.

The lack of uniform interstate recognition of same-sex marriages, civil unions, and domestic partnerships can create difficulties for same-sex couples who seek to dissolve their relationships but who no longer reside—or who never did reside—in the state where the union was entered into. This is because, as a general rule, each state imposes a minimum period of residency—typically between six months and a year—in the state by one spouse prior to filing for divorce in order to establish jurisdiction over the marriage. Although traditionally a requirement only for dissolving marriages, many states with domestic partnerships or civil unions that are identical to marriage impose an identical residency requirement for dissolving such unions.

However, two states that only permit same-sex couples to enter into domestic partnerships or civil unions—Colorado[154] and Oregon[155]— allow domestic partnerships or civil unions entered into those states to be dissolved there even if neither partner resides in the state. In

addition, seven jurisdictions where same-sex marriage is permitted—California,[156] Delaware,[157] the District of Columbia,[158] Hawaii,[159] Illinois,[160] Minnesota,[161] and Vermont[162]—will exercise jurisdiction to divorce the couple if the state where they reside will not recognize the marriage for purposes of granting a divorce.

Local Domestic Partnership Programs

As indicated in Section 1, starting in the mid-1980s, local governments began to enact ordinances creating domestic partnership registries for members of the public-at-large, as well as extending health and other benefits to the same-sex partners of government employees.

As of January 2014, 141 city and county governments have created domestic partnership registries that—while providing virtually no legal benefits—permit same-sex couples to register their relationships. While primarily symbolic in nature, the willingness of local governments in states such as Florida, Georgia, Kansas, Michigan, Minnesota, Montana, Ohio, and Utah—whose statewide laws are generally inhospitable to gays and lesbians—to create these registries provides insight into those areas of the country in which there are pockets of support for gay rights. Map 3 and Table 6 provide detail on these 141 registries, including when they were first enacted.

A much larger number of cities and counties actually extend health and other benefits to the same-sex partners of city and county employees. Some of these jurisdictions go even further, requiring those who do business with the city or county to do the same for the same-sex partners of their employees. (One jurisdiction, while not requiring that such benefits be extended, provides a bidding preference in the contracting process for those that do.) Table 7 and Map 3 detail these programs.

In a few instances, local governments enacted ordinances requiring those doing business with them to provide benefits for the same-sex partners of their employees, but those ordinances were invalidated by either a court or a state legislature. These include New York, New York, whose ordinance was struck down by the New York Court of Appeals; Atlanta, Georgia, whose ordinance was overruled by the Georgia Legislature; and Nashville-Davidson County, Tennessee, whose ordinance was nullified by the Tennessee legislature.

The last few years will go down in history as banner years for enacting domestic partnership ordinances, with 16 ordinances enacted in 2011, 13 ordinances enacted in 2012, and 12 ordinances enacted in 2013. One reason for

Table 5: Interstate recognition of same-sex marriage or other non-marital relationship recognition programs

State	What Will it Recognize
Arizona	Will recognize out-of-state same-sex marriage for purpose of granting an annulment.[163]
California	Out-of-state same-sex marriages performed prior to 11/5/2008 recognized as marriages; other same-sex legal unions recognized as domestic partnerships; marriages performed on or after 11/5/2008 treated in all respects as a marriage except for the use of the term "marriage."[164]
Colorado	Out-of-state same-sex marriages and other unions recognized as civil unions.[165]
Connecticut	Out-of-state same-sex marriages or other relationships that provide substantially the same rights and responsibilities of marriage are recognized as marriage.[166]
Delaware	Out-of-state same-sex marriages and other substantially similar unions recognized as marriage.[167]
Hawaii	Will recognize out-of-state same-sex marriages. Other legal unions between two persons of the same sex are recognized as civil unions.[168]
Illinois	Will recognize out-of-state same-sex marriages. Other legal unions between two persons of the same sex are recognized as civil unions.[169]
Iowa	Generally recognizes out-of-state marriages. No authority on whether it will recognize other types of formalized relationships.[170]
Maine	Will recognize out-of-state same-sex marriages. No authority on whether it will recognize other types of formalized relationships.[171]
Maryland	Out-of-state same-sex marriages will be recognized. No authority on whether it will recognize other types of formalized relationships.[172]
Massachusetts	Out-of-state same-sex marriages as well as other relationships that provide substantially the same rights and responsibilities of marriage are recognized as marriage.[173]
Minnesota	Generally recognizes out-of-state marriages. No authority on whether it will recognize other types of formalized relationships.[174]
Nevada	Legal unions other than marriage that are "substantially equivalent" to domestic partnerships in Nevada are recognized as such, although such unions must still be registered with the state.[175]
New Hampshire	Out-of-state same-sex marriages and civil unions are recognized as marriages. No authority on whether it will recognize other types of formalized relationships.[176]
New Jersey	Will recognize out-of-state same-sex marriages. Legal unions between two persons of the same sex that closely approximate civil unions in New Jersey are recognized as civil unions.[177]
New Mexico	Will recognize out-of-state same-sex marriages. No authority on whether it will recognize other types of formalized relationships.[178]
New York	Out-of-state same-sex marriages and civil unions are recognized. No authority on whether it will recognize other types of formalized relationships.[179]
Ohio	Federal court order requires state to recognize out-of-state same-sex marriages for some purposes.[180]
Oregon	Will recognize out-of-state same-sex marriages. No authority on whether it will recognize other types of formalized relationships.[181]
Rhode Island	Generally recognizes out-of-state marriages. Other unions substantially similar to marriage are recognized as marriage.[182]
Utah	Federal court order (stayed pending appeal) requires state to recognize out-of-state same-sex marriages.[183]
Vermont	Generally recognizes out-of-state marriages. No authority on whether it will recognize other types of formalized relationships.[184]
Washington	Will recognize out-of-state same-sex marriages. Other legal unions that are substantially equivalent to marriage will be temporarily recognized as marriage, but if couple establishes permanent residency in Washington, they must marry within a year.[185]
Washington, D.C.	Out-of-state same-sex marriages are recognized. No authority on whether it will recognize other types of formalized relationships.[186]
Wisconsin	Will not recognize out-of-state marriages or "[a] legal status identical or substantially similar to that of marriage for unmarried individuals."[187]
Wyoming	Recognizes out-of-state same-sex marriages at least for purposes of granting a divorce. No authority on whether it will recognize other types of formalized relationships.[188]

Table 6: Local domestic partnership ordinances, listed by date

Enacted	Jurisdiction	Enacted	Jurisdiction	Enacted	Jurisdiction
1985	West Hollywood, CA	1999	Milwaukee, WI*	2008	Salt Lake City, UT
1990	Ithaca, NY		Olympia, WA	2009	Columbia, MO
	Madison, WI		Petaluma, CA		Duluth, MN
	San Francisco, CA		Santa Barbara Co., CA		St. Paul, MN
1991	Ann Arbor, MI		Tumwater, WA		Yellow Springs, OH
	Berkeley, CA	2000	Lacey, WA	2010	Buffalo, NY
	Minneapolis, MN		Multnomah County, OR		Edina, MN
1992	Cambridge, MA		Palm Springs, CA		Golden Valley, MN
	Laguna Beach, CA	2002	East Hampton, NY		Maplewood, MN
	Sacramento, CA		Eugene, OR		Rochester, MN
1993	Boston, MA		Portland, ME	2011	Asheville, NC*
	Brookline, MA		Westchester Co., NY		Athens, OH
	Hartford, CT	2003	Cook County, IL*		Crystal, MN
	Marin County, CA*		Fulton County, GA*		Falcon Heights, MN
	New Orleans, LA		Great Neck Plaza, NY		Flagstaff, AZ
	New York, NY		Jackson County, MO		Hopkins, MN
	Provincetown, MA		Kansas City, MO		Olivette, MO
	Takoma Park, MD		North Hills, NY		Orlando, FL
	Travis County, TX		Southampton, NY		Red Wing, MN
1994	Carrboro, NC		Southold, NY		Richfield, MN
	Davis, CA		Tucson, AZ		Robbinsdale, MN
	Iowa City, IA	2004	Cleveland Heights, OH*		Saint Louis Park, MN
	Rochester, NY		Great Neck, NY		Shoreview, MN
	Seattle, WA		Huntington, NY		State College, PA
1995	Brewster, MA		Miami Beach, FL		Shorewood, MN
	Chapel Hill, NC		North Hempstead, NY		University City, MO
	Santa Monica, CA		Roslyn Estates, NY	2012	Clayton, MO
1996	Albany, NY		Truro, MA		Clearwater, FL
	Boulder, CO	2005	Urbana, IL		Columbus, OH
	Nantucket, MA		West Palm Beach, FL		Dayton, OH
	Oakland, CA	2006	Athens-Clarke County, GA		Eagan, MN
	Palo Alto, CA		Palm Beach County, FL		Eden Prairie, MN
1997	Atlanta, GA		Rockland County, NY		Gulfport, FL
	Cathedral City, CA		Suffolk County, NY		Northfield, MN
	Long Beach, CA	2007	Eureka Springs, AR		Orange County, FL
	Oak Park, IL*		Gainesville, FL		St. Petersburg, FL
	Santa Barbara City, CA		Lawrence, KS		Sarasota, FL
1998	Arcata, CA		Toledo, OH		Tampa, FL
	Key West, FL	2008	Cleveland, OH		Volusia County, FL
	Philadelphia, PA*		Dane County, WI	2013	Avondale Estates, GA
	St. Louis, MO		Harrisburg, PA		Bisbee, AZ
1999	Ashland, OR*		Ithaca (Town), NY		Decatur, GA
	Broward County, FL		Miami-Dade County, FL		East Lansing, MI
	Denver, CO		Phoenix, AZ		Leon County, FL
	Los Angeles County, CA		Pittsburgh, PA		Missoula, MT

*Open to same-sex couples only.

Table continues, page 19

Map 3

Local domestic partnership registries and equal benefits ordinances

Overview: many local governments offer a form of recognition to same-sex relationships

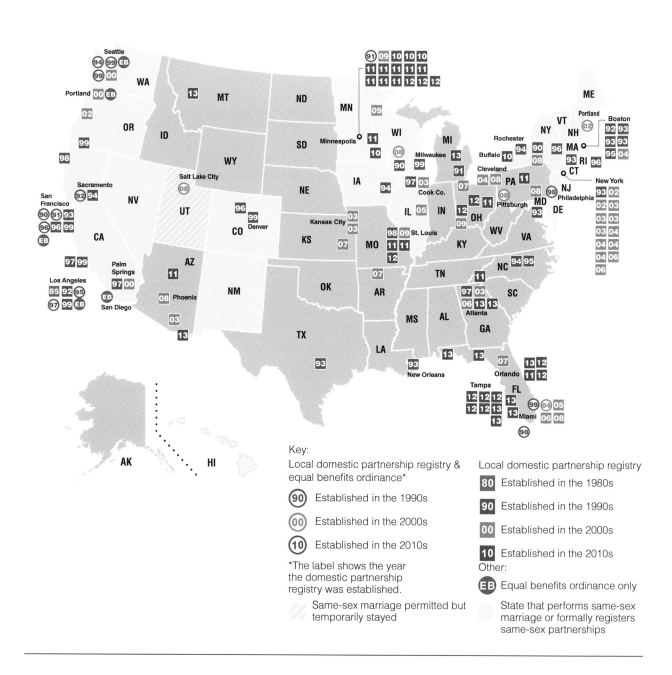

Key:
Local domestic partnership registry & equal benefits ordinance*

(90) Established in the 1990s

(00) Established in the 2000s

(10) Established in the 2010s

*The label shows the year the domestic partnership registry was established.

Same-sex marriage permitted but temporarily stayed

Local domestic partnership registry

80 Established in the 1980s

90 Established in the 1990s

00 Established in the 2000s

10 Established in the 2010s

Other:

EB Equal benefits ordinance only

State that performs same-sex marriage or formally registers same-sex partnerships

Table 6: Local domestic partnership ordinances, listed by date (continued)

Enacted	Jurisdiction
2013 cont'd	North Port, FL
	Pensacola, FL
	Pinellas County, FL
	Sarasota County, FL
	Taveres, FL
	Venice, FL

the increased activity is a concerted effort by proponents of same-sex marriage in two states—Minnesota and Florida—to build grassroots support for same-sex marriage. Of the 41 ordinances enacted in the last three years, 12 were in Minnesota and 15 were in Florida.

Despite advances in marriage equality for same-sex couples, local domestic partnership regestries continue to have strong support. After the U.S. Supreme Court allowed same-sex marriage to resume in California, the Berkeley City Council considered closing the city's long-standing registry, but shelved the proposal after a strong public backlash.

As of January, 2014 an ordinance in Holmes Beach, Florida waits final approval.

Table 7: Equal benefit ordinances

Jurisdiction	Enacted	Details
Berkeley, CA	2001	Equal Benefits Requirement
Broward County, FL*	2011	Equal Benefits Requirement
Dane County, WI	2008	Equal Benefits Requirement
Key West, FL	2012	Equal Benefits Requirement
King County, WA	2003	Equal Benefits Requirement
Long Beach, CA	2009	Equal Benefits Requirement
Los Angeles, CA	1999	Equal Benefits Requirement
Miami Beach, FL	2005	Equal Benefits Requirement
Minneapolis, MN	2002	Equal Benefits Requirement
Oakland, CA	2001	Equal Benefits Requirement
Olympia, WA	2004	Equal Benefits Requirement
Philadelphia, PA	2011	Equal Benefits Requirement
Pittsburgh, PA	2013	Equal Benefits Requirement
Portland, ME	2001	Equal Benefits Requirement**
Portland, OR	2006	Equal Benefits Requirement
Sacramento, CA	2004	Equal Benefits Requirement
Salt Lake City, UT	2004	Half-point bidding preference
San Diego, CA	2010	Equal Benefits Requirement
San Francisco , CA	1996	Equal Benefits Requirement
San Mateo County, CA	2001	Equal Benefits Requirement
Santa Monica, CA	2011	Equal Benefits Requirement
Seattle, WA	1999	Equal Benefits Requirement
Tumwater, WA	2001	Equal Benefits Requirement

*Replaces 1999 1% bidding preference.
**Only for Housing & Community Development fund recipients.

Map 4

1998 - 2012 / Votes regarding same-sex marriage

County-by-county results: most counties approved same-sex marriage bans

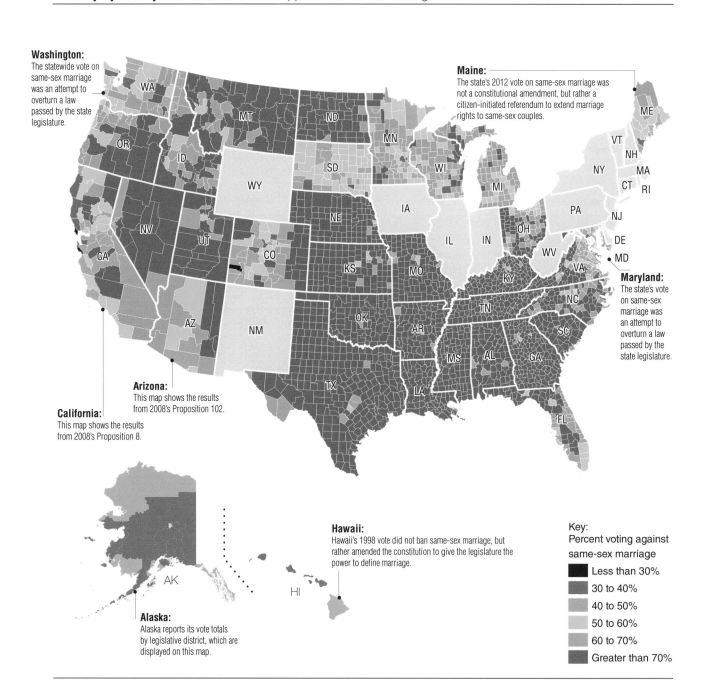

Washington:
The statewide vote on same-sex marriage was an attempt to overturn a law passed by the state legislature.

Maine:
The state's 2012 vote on same-sex marriage was not a constitutional amendment, but rather a citizen-initiated referendum to extend marriage rights to same-sex couples.

Maryland:
The state's vote on same-sex marriage was an attempt to overturn a law passed by the state legislature.

Arizona:
This map shows the results from 2008's Proposition 102.

California:
This map shows the results from 2008's Proposition 8.

Hawaii:
Hawaii's 1998 vote did not ban same-sex marriage, but rather amended the constitution to give the legislature the power to define marriage.

Alaska:
Alaska reports its vote totals by legislative district, which are displayed on this map.

Key:
Percent voting against same-sex marriage

- Less than 30%
- 30 to 40%
- 40 to 50%
- 50 to 60%
- 60 to 70%
- Greater than 70%

3 Same-sex marriage at the ballot box

Starting in 1998, voters in 32 states have been asked to vote on constitutional amendments regarding same-sex marriage. Many of these constitutional amendments banned not only same-sex marriage, but also state recognition of other types of same-sex unions, such as civil unions and domestic partnerships. With the exception of two—Arizona in 2006 and Minnesota in 2012—each of these ballot initiatives has passed. Even in Arizona, two years after a proposed constitutional amendment was rejected by voters, a revised one passed easily. In general, the percentage of voters supporting these initiatives has decreased over time, but has steadily remained over 50 percent.

Figure 3: Population in states where same-sex marriage is prohibited by constitutional amendment

Number of states:	28
Population:	165,911,894
% US population:	53.7%

Source: 2010 Census. Totals exclude Utah.

Figure 3 shows the percentage of the U.S. population living in the 28 states in which same-sex marriage is prohibited by means of a constitutional amendment. It excludes Hawaii, even though Hawaii voters approved an amendment to the state constitution, because it merely gave the legislature the power to define marriage and does not prohibit the state legislature from legalizing same-sex marriage. It also excludes California and Utah, whose constitutional amendments were declared unconstitutional by federal courts. Table 8 ranks the statewide votes on constitutional amendments limiting same-sex marriage based on the margin by which they passed.

Table 9 includes all statewide votes on the issue of same-sex marriage, not just consitutional amendments. It thus includes votes in Maine, Maryland and Washington approving or rejecting the right of same-sex couples to marry, as well as a 2000 vote enacting a statutory ban on same-sex marriages in California. The table provides a detailed look at each of these votes. Map 4 switches the

Table 8: Statewide votes on constitutional amendments limiting same-sex marriage, ranked by percent voting yes

Rank & State	Year	Yes %	No %
1. Mississippi	2004	86%	14%
2. Tennessee	2006	81%	19%
3. Alabama	2006	81%	19%
4. South Carolina	2006	78%	22%
5. Louisiana	2004	78%	22%
6. Texas	2005	76%	24%
7. Georgia	2004	76%	24%
8. Oklahoma	2004	76%	24%
9. Arkansas	2004	75%	25%
10. Kentucky	2004	75%	25%
11. North Dakota	2004	73%	27%
12. Hawaii	1998	71%	29%
13. Missouri	2004	71%	29%
14. Nebraska	2000	70%	30%
15. Kansas	2005	70%	30%
16. Alaska	1998	68%	32%
17. Nevada	2002	67%	33%
18. Montana	2004	67%	33%
19. Utah	2004	66%	34%
20. Idaho	2006	63%	37%
21. Florida	2008	62%	38%
22. Ohio	2004	62%	38%
23. North Carolina	2000	61%	39%
24. Wisconsin	2006	59%	41%
25. Michigan	2004	59%	41%
26. Virginia	2006	57%	43%
27. Oregon	2004	57%	43%
28. Arizona	2008	56%	44%
29. Colorado	2006	55%	45%
30. California	2008	52%	48%
31. South Dakota	2006	52%	48%
32. Arizona	2006	48%	52%
33. Minnesota	2012	47%	53%

Source: Secretary of State's Office in each state

Table 9: All statewide votes on same-sex marriage

Year	State	Description of Vote	Month of Vote	Yes Votes	No Votes	Yes %	No %	Constitutional Amendment?
1998	Alaska	Ban marriage	November	152,965	71,631	68%	32%	Yes
1998	Hawaii	Marriage ban authorized	November	285,384	117,827	71%	29%	Yes
2000	California	Ban marriage	March	4,618,673	2,909,370	61%	39%	No
2000	Nebraska	Ban marriage/other unions	November	477,571	203,667	70%	30%	Yes
2002	Nevada	Ban marriage	November	337,197	164,573	67%	33%	Yes
2004	Arkansas	Ban marriage/other unions	November	753,770	251,914	75%	25%	Yes
2004	Georgia	Ban marriage/other unions	November	2,454,930	768,716	76%	24%	Yes
2004	Kentucky	Ban marriage/other unions	November	1,222,125	417,097	75%	25%	Yes
2004	Louisiana	Ban marriage/other unions	September	619,908	177,067	78%	22%	Yes
2004	Michigan	Ban marriage/other unions	November	2,698,077	1,904,319	59%	41%	Yes
2004	Mississippi	Ban marriage	November	957,104	155,648	86%	14%	Yes
2004	Missouri	Ban marriage	August	1,055,771	439,529	71%	29%	Yes
2004	Montana	Ban marriage	November	295,070	148,263	67%	33%	Yes
2004	North Dakota	Ban marriage/other unions	November	223,572	81,716	73%	27%	Yes
2004	Ohio	Ban marriage/other unions	November	3,329,335	2,065,462	62%	38%	Yes
2004	Oklahoma	Ban marriage/other unions[189]	November	1,075,216	347,303	76%	24%	Yes
2004	Oregon	Ban marriage	November	1,028,546	787,556	57%	43%	Yes
2004	Utah	Ban marriage/other unions	November	593,297	307,488	66%	34%	Yes
2005	Kansas	Ban marriage/other unions	April	417,627	179,432	70%	30%	Yes
2005	Texas	Ban marriage/other unions	November	1,723,782	536,913	76%	24%	Yes
2006	Alabama	Ban marriage/other unions	June	697,591	161,694	81%	19%	Yes
2006	Arizona	Ban marriage/other unions	November	721,489	775,498	48%	52%	Yes
2006	Colorado	Ban marriage	November	855,126	699,030	55%	45%	Yes
2006	Idaho	Ban marriage/other unions	November	282,386	163,384	63%	37%	Yes
2006	South Carolina	Ban marriage/other unions	November	829,360	234,316	78%	22%	Yes
2006	South Dakota	Ban marriage/other unions	November	172,305	160,152	52%	48%	Yes
2006	Tennessee	Ban marriage	November	1,419,434	327,536	81%	19%	Yes
2006	Virginia	Ban marriage/other unions	November	1,328,537	999,687	57%	43%	Yes
2006	Wisconsin	Ban marriage/other unions	November	1,264,310	862,924	59%	41%	Yes
2008	Arizona	Ban marriage	November	1,258,355	980,753	56%	44%	Yes
2008	California	Ban marriage	November	7,001,084	6,401,482	52%	48%	Yes
2008	Florida	Ban marriage/other unions	November	4,890,883	3,008,026	62%	38%	Yes
2009	Maine	Veto marriage equality law	November	300,848	267,828	53%	47%	No
2012	North Carolina	Ban marriage/other unions	May	1,317,178	840,802	61%	39%	Yes
2012	Maine	Permit marriage	November	372,887	334,723	53%	47%	No
2012	Maryland	Permit marriage	November	1,373,504	1,246,045	52%	48%	No
2012	Minnesota*	Ban Marriage	November	1,399,916	1,550,864	47%	53%	Yes
2012	Washington	Permit marriage	November	1,659,915	1,431,285	54%	46%	No

*The number and percentage of No votes in Minnesota includes blank votes, which are treated as No votes.

Table 10: Where did efforts to ban same-sex marriage by constitutional amendment have the LEAST support?

Rank & Jurisdiction	Population (2010)	Yes %	No %
1. Orange, NC	133,801	21%	79%
2. Charlottesville, VA	43,475	23%	77%
3. San Francisco, CA	805,235	25%	75%
4. Marin, CA	252,409	25%	75%
5. Arlington, VA	207,627	26%	74%
6. Santa Cruz, CA	262,382	29%	71%
7. San Miguel, CO	7,359	29%	71%
8. Alexandria, VA	139,966	30%	70%
9. Pitkin, CO	17,148	30%	70%
10. Durham, NC	267,587	30%	70%
11. Richmond City, VA	204,214	30%	70%
12. Falls Church, VA	12,332	31%	69%
13. Dane, WI	488,073	33%	67%
14. Boulder, CO	294,567	33%	67%
15. Sonoma, CA	483,878	34%	66%
16. Blaine, ID	21,376	34%	66%
17. Clay, SD	13,864	35%	65%
18. Petersburg, VA	32,420	35%	65%
19. Shannon, SD	13,586	35%	65%
20. Hennepin, MN	1,152,425	35%	65%

Table 11: Where did efforts to ban same-sex marriage by constitutional amendment have the MOST support?

Rank & Jurisdiction	Population (2010)	Yes %	No %
1. Martin, TX	4,799	95%	5%
2. Floyd, TX	6,446	95%	5%
3. Parmer, TX	10,269	95%	5%
4. Ochiltree, TX	10,223	95%	5%
5. Hansford, TX	5,613	95%	5%
6. Garza, TX	6,461	95%	5%
7. Childress, TX	7,041	95%	5%
8. Motley, TX	1,210	95%	5%
9. Dallam, TX	6,703	94%	6%
10. Hartley, TX	6,062	94%	6%
11. Lipscomb, TX	3,302	94%	6%
12. Itawamba, MS	23,401	94%	6%
13. Wheeler, TX	5,410	94%	6%
14. Gaines, TX	17,526	94%	6%
15. La Salle, LA	14,890	94%	6%
16. Pontotoc, MS	29,957	94%	6%
17. Briscoe, TX	1,637	94%	6%
18. Magoffin, KY	13,333	94%	6%
19. Hardin, TX	54,635	94%	6%
20. Pierce, GA	18,758	94%	6%

focus from states to the local level, showing the relative support for same-sex marriage. Tables 10 and 11 are limited to constitutional amendments, and show the jurisdictions where bans were least and most popular.

While it is no surprise to see some familiar liberal counties from California on the list of places where support for constitutional amendments was weakest, it may be surprising that counties from states such as Idaho, South Dakota, and Virginia appear there as well. In Virginia, many cities are separate legal entities from the surrounding counties. In general, voters in cities were more likely to oppose these amendments. Blaine County, Idaho is the home of affluent Sun Valley, while Clay County, South Dakota is the home of the University of South Dakota.

Many of the counties where support for constitutional amendments was most popular are located in Texas, where counties tend to be small and often, relatively homogeneous. Counties in Mississippi, Louisiana,

Kentucky, and Georgia also appear on the list.

The process of amending state constitutions

As shown above, 31 states have amended their constitutions to limit same-sex marriage. Why haven't the other 19 states followed suit? While the answer may turn in part on political demographics within each state, some of it may be explained by the ease or difficulty with which state constitutions can be amended in each of the states.

For example, 16 of the 31 states that have amended their constitutions have a procedure by which constitutional amendments can be placed on the ballot by means of a citizen-initiated signature-gathering process, without any role for the legislature to play. In contrast, *none* of the states that lack marriage amendments to their constitutions allow their constitutions to be amended without the support of some percentage of the state legislature. Accordingly, in these states, the legislature

Table 12: State Constitutional Amendment Procedures

State	Citizen-Initiated Amendment Procedure	Legislative Supermajority	Successive Session Requirement	Automatic Constitutional Convention Vote	Voter Supermajority
Connecticut	No	Yes (3/4)[190]	Yes[190]	Every 20 years (2028)	No
Delaware	No	Yes (2/3)	Yes	No	n/a[191]
Illinois	No[192]	Yes (3/5)	No	Every 20 years (2028)	Yes (3/5)[193]
Indiana	No	No	Yes	No	No
Iowa	No	No	Yes	Every 10 years (2020)	No
Maine	No	Yes (2/3)	No	No	No
Maryland	No	Yes (3/5)	No	Every 20 years (2020)	No
Massachusetts	Yes[194]	No	Yes	No	No
Minnesota	No	No	No	No	Yes[195]
New Hampshire	No	Yes (3/5)	No	Every 10 years (2022)	Yes (2/3)
New Jersey	No	Yes (3/5)[196]	Yes[196]	No	No
New Mexico	No	No	No	No	No
New York	No	No	Yes	Every 20 years (2017)	No
Pennsylvania	No	No	Yes	No	No
Rhode Island	No	No	No	Every 10 years (2014)	No
Vermont	No	Yes (2/3)[197]	No	No	No
Washington	No	Yes (2/3)	No	No	No
West Virginia	No	Yes (2/3)	No	No	No
Wyoming	No	Yes (2/3)	No	No	Yes[195]

serves as a sort of buffer between the passions of one group of citizens and the rights of another.

Moreover the constitutions of many of these 19 states contain one or both of the following, additional hurdles to amending the constitution: a legislative supermajority requirement, and a successive session requirement. The legislative supermajority requirement allows a constitutional amendment to appear before voters only if a significant percentage of each house of the legislature—anywhere from 60 to 75 percent (3/5 to 3/4)—vote in favor of it, thus providing greater protection for minority rights. The successive session requirement allows a constitutional amendment to appear before voters only if the legislature approves it by the requisite percentage in two successive legislative sessions, thus effectively providing for a mandatory "cooling off" period, during which passions may wane. In addition, a handful of these states also require that the amendment be approved by more than just a simple majority of voters.

While these various hurdles can provide some protection against constitutional amendments, they are not insurmountable: 15 of the 31 states that have amended their constitutions lack a procedure for citizen-initiated constitutional amendments and have either a legislative supermajority requirement, a successive session requirement, or both.

Moreover, even in states that contain these various hurdles to making specific constitutional amendments, there remains a second route to constitutional amendment: the calling of a constitutional convention, at which all aspects of the constitution are on the table. Of the 19 states that lack marriage amendments, 7 have provisions that give citizens the right to automatically vote on whether to hold a constitutional convention at specified intervals of time. Table 12 provides detail on the presence or absence of these various hurdles to constitutional amendment in the 19 states that currently lack marriage amendments. This explains why recent efforts to amend state constitutions in Iowa and Wyoming stalled. Wyoming requires a two-thirds legislative supermajority, while Iowa requires approval by successive sessions of the legislature.

4 Notable statewide votes

Several statewide votes related to same-sex marriage and relationship recognition deserve a closer look. The pages that follow accordingly provide a detailed analysis of votes that took place in the states of Arizona, California, Colorado, Maine, Maryland and Washington.

Arizona

Arizona voters rejected a constitutional amendment in 2006, but changed their mind two years later. The vote is analyzed in detail in Maps 5 and 6.

Proposition 107: In 2006, several states voted on constitutional amendments prohibiting same-sex marriage. All of these measures passed, with the exception of Arizona's. State voters handed religious conservatives a surprising defeat by rejecting the proposed amendment at the ballot box, the first time this ever happened.

One of the main reasons behind the defeat of the ballot measure was the provision banning other unions, such as civil unions and domestic partnerships. Many senior citizens opposed the amendment for this reason, possibly hoping to take advantage of such a program in the future. Civil unions and domestic partnerships are popular with seniors as they extend the protections of marriage without some of the negative financial consequences. Marriage between seniors could reduce a couple's Social Security benefits, whereas civil unions or domestic partnerships (unrecognized by the federal government) would not. In fact, much of the campaign against the amendment did not even focus on same-sex couples, but instead focused on the impact it would have on heterosexual seniors.

Another factor that may have contributed to the failure of Proposition 107 was the fact that 2006 was generally a difficult election year for conservative candidates and their causes, with independent voters rejecting some of the policies of the George W. Bush administration and some disillusioned "values" voters sitting the election out.

Proposition 102: In 2008, another amendment was put before voters, this time without the provision banning other unions. Removing this provision probably ensured the passage of this ballot measure, since many senior citizens voted against the 2006 measure because of its ban on other unions. The 2008 amendment passed easily, winning in all but Pima County, the location of Tucson.

Two other factors likely contributed to Proposition 102's success. First, in neighboring California, the California Supreme Court had struck down the state's ban on same-sex marriage in May, and same-sex couples began to legally wed there. The pro-Proposition 102 campaign repeatedly pointed to the California Supreme Court's decision as a reason Arizona needed a constitutional amendment. Second, 2008 was a presidential election year, with a large general turnout. The Republican candidate on the ballot, John McCain, was the favorite son of Arizona, having represented that state in Congress for decades; this undoubtedly increased conservative turnout.

California

California voters also voted twice on banning same-sex marriage, in 2000 on a state law, then again in 2008 on a constitutional amendment. The differences between the two votes are analyzed in detail in Maps 7 and 8.

Proposition 22: In 2000, Californians voted on a measure prohibiting same-sex marriages, making it only the third state in which voters were asked to decide this issue. The California measure was not a constitutional amendment, however, but rather a citizen-initiated law, and it was overturned in 2008 by the California Supreme Court as violative of the California Constitution.

Proposition 22 did well statewide, passing with over 60 percent of the vote. With the exception of a few counties in and near the Bay Area, the proposition passed in all other counties. Several factors explain the healthy margin by which Proposition 22 was approved. First, it took place during a primary election in March rather than a general election in November, and thus had a much lower participation rate. Second, in 2000, there were no legally wed same-sex couples in California or indeed anywhere else in the United States, and so voters were not being asked to take away a pre-existing right from anyone.

Proposition 8: In May 2008, the California Supreme Court ruled that the 2000 voter approved law limiting marriage to opposite-sex couples violated the California Constitution. The state was forced to recognize same-sex marriages, and such marriages began taking place later that month. The ruling sprang from litigation surrounding the City and County of San Francisco's decision to grant marriage licenses to same-sex couples.

The campaign to get Proposition 8 on the ballot and to collect signatures began in October 2007, long before the May 2008 California Supreme Court decision. After a brief but expensive campaign, the amendment was approved by voters in the November 2008 general election.

The racial aspect of the vote was noteworthy. According to an analysis by the New York Times, under 50 percent of whites voted yes, while over 50 percent of Latina/os and approximately 70 percent of African-Americans voted yes.[198] The heavy vote for the amendment by African-American voters graphically illustrates the community's unease with same-sex marriage. On average, African-American voters tend to be more religious than whites, and leaders of many African-American churches are vocal opponents of same-sex marriage.

Geographically, the opposition to the amendment was greatest in the Bay Area and other counties along the coast. The measure also failed in two rural counties in the Sierra Nevada Mountains, Alpine and Mono. The Amendment passed in Los Angeles County—the state's most populous—as well as Orange, San Diego and Sacramento Counties. It also passed easily in Riverside County, home to the large Palm Springs gay community.

The outcome of the election left same-sex couples in California in a strange situation: a subsequent California Supreme Court decision held that same-sex marriages that occurred between May and the November 2008 election remained legal and valid, but that no new same-sex couples were permitted to marry. Not until June, 2013—when the U.S. Supreme Court held that supporters of Proposition 8 lacked standing to appeal a federal court decision declaring it unconstitutional—did same-sex marriages resume in that state.

Colorado

Colorado voters rejected efforts to establish a statewide domestic partnership registry in 2006. The details of this fairly close vote are analyzed in Map 9.

The measure—dubbed Referendum I—failed, although not by a great margin. Geographically, it passed easily in Denver, Boulder and some of the affluent counties in the Rocky Mountains, including Pitkin—the location of Aspen—and San Miguel—the location of Telluride.

While this referendum failed, in 2009 the Colorado Legislature did enact legislation giving same-sex couples some legal protections. The program, entitled designated beneficiaries, is not limited to same-sex couples, and provides a much more limited set of rights than Referendum I would have provided. In 2013, a bill enacting civil unions for same-sex couples was approved by the state's legislature and signed into law by its governor.

Maine

Voters in Maine in 2009 voted to overturn a law extending marriage rights to same-sex couples, but 3 years later reversed course and voted to extend such rights to same-sex couples. The results of these two close elections are analyzed in Maps 10 and 11.

In 2009, the Maine Legislature approved a law legalizing same-sex marriage. However, a citizen group launched a successful campaign that placed the measure in front of state voters. A "yes" vote on the measure—entitled Question 1—was a vote to repeal the law legalizing same-sex marriage. Geographically, the measure did poorly in Portland, the state's largest city, and a few coastal counties, but passed easily in most other parts of the state. As a result, by a narrow margin, voters in Maine decided to exercise a citizens' veto of the legislation, and thus the law legalizing same-sex marriage never went into effect. The state's pre-existing domestic partnership program continued to exist, however, giving same-sex couples at least a modest degree of legal protection.

Maine's Question 1 was not a constitutional amendment, but rather a veto of legislative action, leaving open the possibility that marriage rights could subsequently be extended to same-sex couples. Three years later, supporters of same-sex marriage bypassed the legislature and collected enough signatures to place the issue directly before voters. The 2012 measure—also dubbed Question 1—was approved by a narrow margin, with a "yes" vote on this measure signifying a vote to approve same-sex marriage. The margin of victory was provided by counties on Maine's southern coast, with three counties that narrowly rejected marriage rights in 2009—Lincoln, Sagadahoc, and Waldo—voting to approve them in 2012.

This was not the first time that voters in Maine had a change of heart on a question related to gay rights. A number of years earlier, voters in Maine voted to reject a law enacted by the legislature adding sexual orientation to the state's anti-discrimination laws, only to reverse course a few years later and vote to approve such a law.

Maryland

Voters in Maryland in 2012 voted to approve a law enacted by the state legislature extending marriage rights to same-sex couples. The results of this close election are analyzed in Map 12.

In 2012, Maryland's legislature voted to extend marriage rights to same-sex couples, and the state's governor signed the bill into law. The bill was set to take effect in January 2013 so as to give opponents a chance to seek a public vote on the measure before it took effect. Opponents collected enough signatures to place the issue before voters in the November 2012 election.

The measure—entitled Question 6—asked citizens to approve or reject the new law, with a "yes" vote on the measure signifying a vote to approve same-sex marriage. African Americans—who represent 30 percent of the state's population—were a major voting bloc coveted by both supporters and opponents of same-sex marriage. While some African-American leaders, most notably President Obama, campaigned in support of same-sex marriage in the state, leaders of many of the state's African-American churches came out strongly against it. The measure narrowly failed in Prince Georges County— where African Americans represent nearly two-thirds of the population—but the measure nonetheless succeeded as a result of strong support in both the Baltimore area and in progressive Montgomery County, which abuts Washington, D.C.

Washington

Washington voters twice rejected efforts by conservative groups to prevent laws enacted by the state legislature expanding relationship recognition rights for same-sex couples from taking effect. In so doing, Washington in 2009 became the first state ever to approve such rights in a statewide vote, and in 2012 became the first state ever to do so more than once. The results of these two elections are analyzed in Maps 13 and 14.

Washington's legislature first enacted a modest domestic partnership program with only a handful of rights in 2007. In 2008 the legislature voted to add numerous additional rights, and in 2009 it voted to expand the program to include all of the rights associated with marriage. The law covered same-sex couples as well as senior citizens. Washington state law gives citizens the right to put newly enacted laws to a public vote if a certain number of signatures are gathered. Religious groups mounted a campaign to prevent the "all but marriage" law from taking effect. While the number of valid signatures gathered was fairly close to the minimum number required, the measure was certified for the November 2009 ballot.

As a challenge to a newly enacted law, the measure— entitled Referendum 71—asked citizens to approve or reject the expanded domestic partnership law. Thus, a "yes" vote on the measure was a vote to expand the domestic partnership program. The groups in favor of the expanded legislation launched a campaign for voters to approve it, bolstered by donations from the state's large business community, including Microsoft and Boeing.

In the end, Washington voters approved the legislation, led by an enormous margin in Seattle and King County, the state's most populous city and county, respectively. Somewhat surprisingly, the measure also passed in more rural counties in the northwest portion of the state. Voters in more conservative eastern Washington and southwest Washington voted against the measure, but not by enough to overcome the strong yes vote in the Puget Sound area.

In 2012, the Washington Legislature voted to extend full marriage rights to same-sex couples. Once again, religious groups mounted a campaign to block the law from taking effect. This time, their campaign was far more organized and better funded, and they turned in twice the required number of signatures necessary to force a public vote on the issue.

The 2012 measure—entitled Referendum 74—asked citizens to approve or reject marriage rights for same-sex couples, with a "yes" vote on the measure translating into support for marriage rights. The measure was ap-proved by a slightly larger margin than Referendum 71, an impressive outcome given that it was about marriage. Supporters of marriage rights were well organized and very well-funded, with Amazon CEO Jeff Bezos and his wife alone donating 2.5 million dollars to the campaign. The campaign mounted an effective advertising campaign that featured religious officials, Republican legislators, and friends and family members of gays and lesbians explaining the importance of approving marriage rights for same-sex couples.

Arizona

Map 5 - 2006 / **Proposition 107**

Apache, Coconino and Navajo Counties: These counties are home to the Hopi and Navajo nations.

Maricopa County: Location of Phoenix, the most populous county in the state.

Rejected: constitutional amendment prohibiting same-sex marriage and other unions

Summary:
Election Date: November 7, 2006

Yes: 48.2%
No: 51.8%

Yes votes: 721,489
No votes: 775,498

Map Key:
Percent voting Yes
- Less than 45%
- 45 to 50%
- 50 to 55%
- 55 to 60%
- Greater than 60%

⬇ Lowest % of yes votes:
Coconino [40%]

⬆ Highest % of yes votes:
Graham [69%]

Map 6 - 2008 / **Proposition 102**

Pima County: Location of Tucson, the state's second largest city, and the University of Arizona.

Approved: constitutional amendment prohibiting same-sex marriage

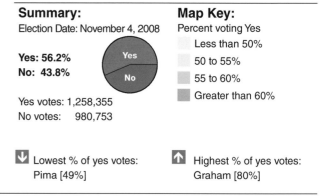

Summary:
Election Date: November 4, 2008

Yes: 56.2%
No: 43.8%

Yes votes: 1,258,355
No votes: 980,753

Map Key:
Percent voting Yes
- Less than 50%
- 50 to 55%
- 55 to 60%
- Greater than 60%

⬇ Lowest % of yes votes:
Pima [49%]

⬆ Highest % of yes votes:
Graham [80%]

California

Map 7 - 2000 / **Proposition 22**

Map 8 - 2008 / **Proposition 8**

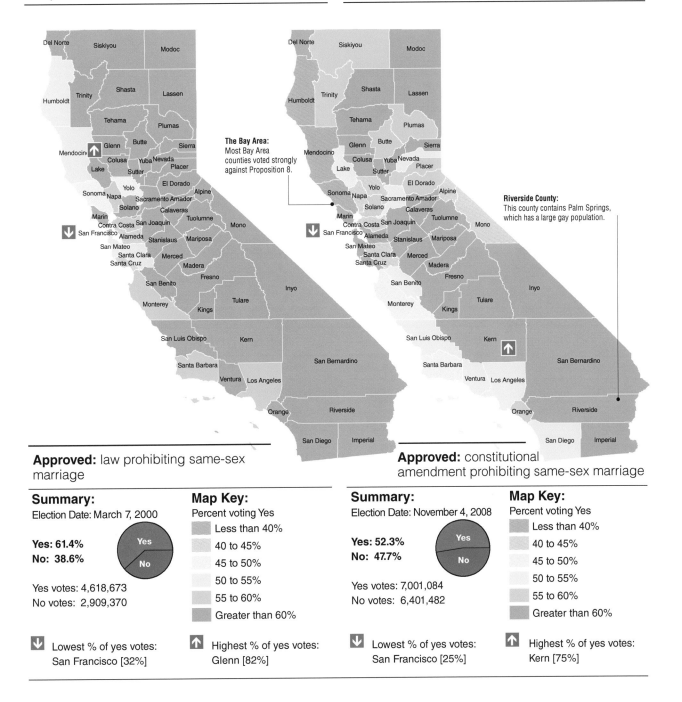

The Bay Area:
Most Bay Area counties voted strongly against Proposition 8.

Riverside County:
This county contains Palm Springs, which has a large gay population.

Approved: law prohibiting same-sex marriage

Approved: constitutional amendment prohibiting same-sex marriage

Summary:
Election Date: March 7, 2000

Yes: 61.4%
No: 38.6%

Yes votes: 4,618,673
No votes: 2,909,370

Map Key:
Percent voting Yes

- Less than 40%
- 40 to 45%
- 45 to 50%
- 50 to 55%
- 55 to 60%
- Greater than 60%

Lowest % of yes votes:
San Francisco [32%]

Highest % of yes votes:
Glenn [82%]

Summary:
Election Date: November 4, 2008

Yes: 52.3%
No: 47.7%

Yes votes: 7,001,084
No votes: 6,401,482

Map Key:
Percent voting Yes

- Less than 40%
- 40 to 45%
- 45 to 50%
- 50 to 55%
- 55 to 60%
- Greater than 60%

Lowest % of yes votes:
San Francisco [25%]

Highest % of yes votes:
Kern [75%]

Colorado

Map 9 - 2006 / **Referendum I**

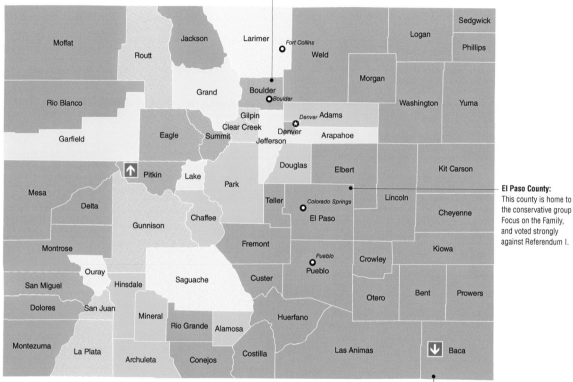

Denver and Boulder Counties: Both of these counties have large urban populations and a large percentage of yes votes.

El Paso County: This county is home to the conservative group Focus on the Family, and voted strongly against Referendum I.

Southeastern Colorado: Some of the highest percentage of No votes occured in counties in the southeastern part of the state, which borders Oklahoma and Kansas.

Rejected: proposition creating a statewide domestic partnership program

Summary:
Election Date: November 7, 2006

Yes: 47.7%
No: 52.3%

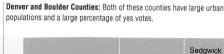

Yes votes: 734,385
No votes: 806,717

Map Key:
Percent voting Yes

- Less than 40%
- 40 to 45%
- 45 to 50%
- 50 to 55%
- 55 to 60%
- Greater than 60%

⬇ Lowest % of yes votes:
Baca [15%]

⬆ Highest % of yes votes:
Pitkin [76%]

Maine

Map 10 - 2009 / **Question 1**

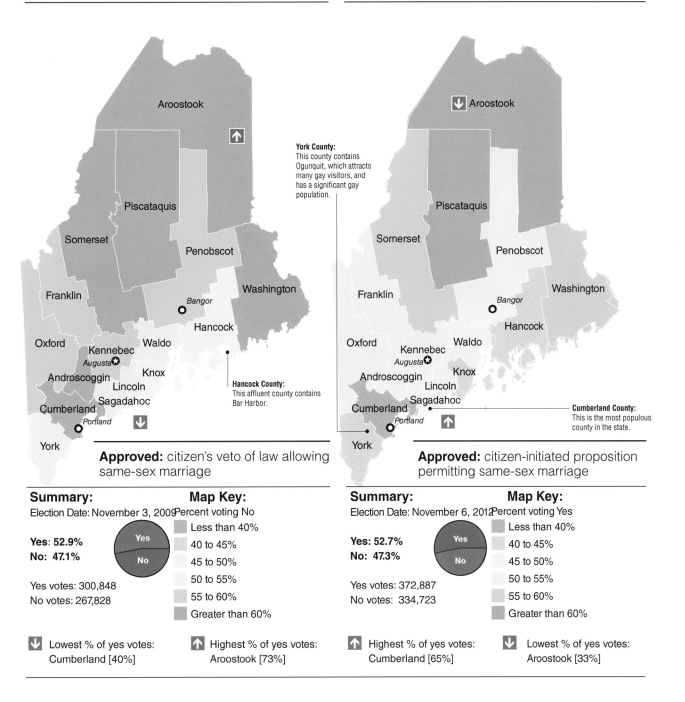

Approved: citizen's veto of law allowing same-sex marriage

York County:
This county contains Ogunquit, which attracts many gay visitors, and has a significant gay population.

Hancock County:
This affluent county contains Bar Harbor.

Summary:
Election Date: November 3, 2009

Yes: 52.9%
No: 47.1%

Yes votes: 300,848
No votes: 267,828

Map Key:
Percent voting No
- Less than 40%
- 40 to 45%
- 45 to 50%
- 50 to 55%
- 55 to 60%
- Greater than 60%

⬇ Lowest % of yes votes:
Cumberland [40%]

⬆ Highest % of yes votes:
Aroostook [73%]

Map 11 - 2012 / **Question 1**

Approved: citizen-initiated proposition permitting same-sex marriage

Cumberland County:
This is the most populous county in the state.

Summary:
Election Date: November 6, 2012

Yes: 52.7%
No: 47.3%

Yes votes: 372,887
No votes: 334,723

Map Key:
Percent voting Yes
- Less than 40%
- 40 to 45%
- 45 to 50%
- 50 to 55%
- 55 to 60%
- Greater than 60%

⬆ Highest % of yes votes:
Cumberland [65%]

⬇ Lowest % of yes votes:
Aroostook [33%]

Maryland

Map 12 - 2012 / **Question 6**

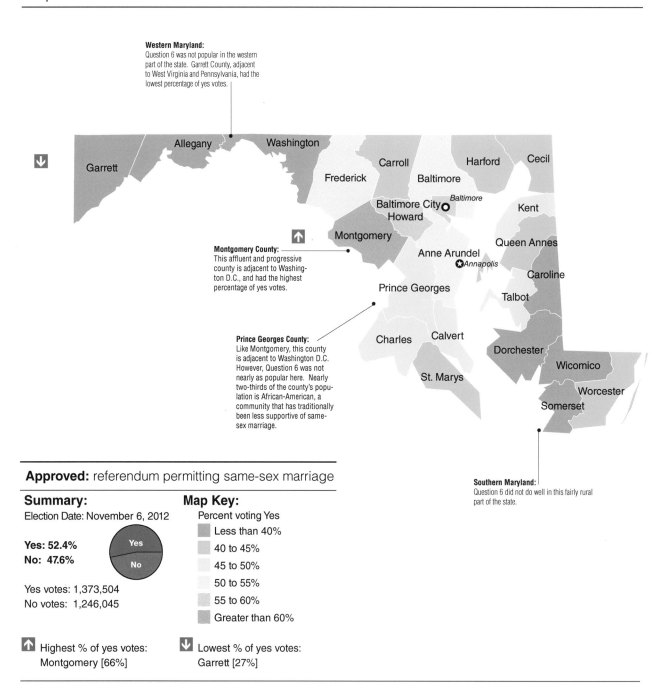

Western Maryland:
Question 6 was not popular in the western part of the state. Garrett County, adjacent to West Virginia and Pennsylvania, had the lowest percentage of yes votes.

Montgomery County:
This affluent and progressive county is adjacent to Washington D.C., and had the highest percentage of yes votes.

Prince Georges County:
Like Montgomery, this county is adjacent to Washington D.C. However, Question 6 was not nearly as popular here. Nearly two-thirds of the county's population is African-American, a community that has traditionally been less supportive of same-sex marriage.

Southern Maryland:
Question 6 did not do well in this fairly rural part of the state.

Approved: referendum permitting same-sex marriage

Summary:
Election Date: November 6, 2012

Yes: 52.4%
No: 47.6%

Yes votes: 1,373,504
No votes: 1,246,045

Map Key:
Percent voting Yes

- Less than 40%
- 40 to 45%
- 45 to 50%
- 50 to 55%
- 55 to 60%
- Greater than 60%

↑ Highest % of yes votes:
Montgomery [66%]

↓ Lowest % of yes votes:
Garrett [27%]

Washington

Map 13 - 2009 / **Referendum 71**

Lowest % of yes votes:
Garfield [23%]

Highest % of yes votes:
San Juan [71%]

Approved: referendum expanding the state's existing domestic partnership program

Summary:
Election Date: November 3, 2009

Yes: 53.2%
No: 46.8%

Yes votes: 951,822
No votes: 838,842

Map Key:
Percent voting Yes
- Less than 40%
- 40 to 45%
- 45 to 50%
- 50 to 55%
- 55 to 60%
- Greater than 60%

Map 14 - 2012 / **Referendum 74**

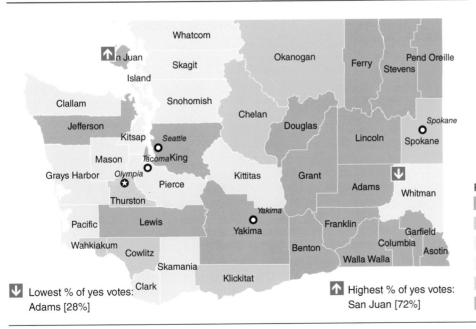

Lowest % of yes votes:
Adams [28%]

Highest % of yes votes:
San Juan [72%]

Approved: referendum permitting same-sex marriage

Summary:
Election Date: November 6, 2012

Yes: 53.7%
No: 46.3%

Yes votes: 1,659,915
No votes: 1,431,285

Map Key:
Percent voting Yes
- Less than 40%
- 40 to 45%
- 45 to 50%
- 50 to 55%
- 55 to 60%
- Greater than 60%

Endnotes

1   At about the same time as the Minnesota litigation, a lower court in New York held a marriage between two people who were of the same sex at the time the marriage was entered into invalid under New York law. The decision did not address any constitutional claims. *See* Anonymous v. Anonymous, 67 Misc. 2d 982 (N.Y. Sup. Ct. 1971).

2   *See* McConell v. Anderson, 451 F.2d 193, 195 (8th Cir. 1971).

3   *See* Baker v. Nelson, 191 N.W.2d 185 (Minn. 1971).

4   *See* Baker v. Nelson, 409 U.S. 810 (1972).

5   *See* Jones v. Hallahan, 501 S.W.2d 588 (Ky. 1973).

6   *See* Singer v. Hara, 522 P.2d 1187 (Wash. 1974).

7   During that same period, a federal court challenge was brought in Wisconsin but subsequently abandoned by the plaintiffs before the court could issue a decision. *See* Burkett v. Zablocki, 54 F.R.D. 626 (E.D. Wis. 1972).

8   *See* Singer v. U.S. Civil Service Com'n, 530 F.2d 247 (9th Cir. 1976); McConnell v. Anderson, 451 F.2d 193 (8th Cir. 1971).

9   *See* Adams v. Howerton, 486 F. Supp. 1119 (C.D. Cal. 1980), *aff'd* 673 F.2d 1036 (9th Cir. 1982).

10   *See* Irwin v. Lupardus, 1980 WL 355015 (Ohio Ct. App. Jun. 26, 1980).

11   *See* DeSanto v. Barnsley, 35 Pa. D. & C.3d 7 (1982), *aff'd*, 476 A.2d 952 (Pa. Super. Ct. 1984).

12   Around this same period, a lower New York court refused to let one same-sex partner legally adopt the other in an effort to obtain some form of legal recognition of their relationship. *See In re* Robert P., 117 Misc.2d 279 (N.Y. Fam. Ct. 1983).

13   Although the City of Berkeley was the first in the nation to enact a domestic partnership ordinance, the initial ordinance did not permit members of the public-at-large to register as domestic partners, but only extended benefits to employees in same-sex relationships. The City of West Hollywood was the first to enact a domestic partnership registry in 1985, with Berkeley not enacting one until 1991. *See* Ryan M. Deam, *Creating the Perfect Case: The Constitutionality of Retroactive Application of the Domestic Partner Rights and Responsibilities Act of 2003*, 35 Pepp. L. Rev. 733, 741-42 (2008); Leland Traiman, *A Brief History of Domestic Partnerships*, Gay & Lesbian Review (July-August 2008).

14   *See* Craig A. Bowman & Blake M. Cornish, *A More Perfect Union: A Legal and Social Analysis of Domestic Partnership Ordinances*, 92 Colum. L. Rev. 1164, 1188-89 (1992).

15   *See* Braschi v. Stahl Associates Co., 74 N.Y.2d 201 (1989).

16   *See In re* Cooper, 149 Misc.2d 282 (N.Y. Surr. Ct. 1990), *aff'd* 187 A.D.2d 128 (N.Y. App. Div. 1993).

17   *See* Dean v. District of Columbia, 1992 WL 685364 (D.C. Super. Ct. 1992), *aff'd* 653 A.2d 307 (D.C. 1995).

18   *See* Baehr v. Lewin, 852 P.2d 44 (Haw. 1993).

19   *See* Pub. L. 104-199, Sept. 21, 1996, 110 Stat. 2419.

20   517 U.S. 620 (1996).

21   *See* 1997 Hawaii Laws Act 383 (H.B. 118).

22   *See* Brause v. Bureau of Vital Statistics, 1998 WL 88743 (Alaska Super. Ct. 1998).

23   *See* Baker v. State, 744 A.2d 864 (Vt. 1999).

24   *See* 2000 Vt. Laws P.A. 91 (H. 847).

25   *See Baker*, 744 A.2d at 204 n.5; *id.* at 243 n.2 (Johnson, J., concurring in part and dissenting in part).

26   *See* Tanner v. OHSU, 971 P.2d 435 (Or. Ct. App. 1998).

27   *See* 1999 Cal. Legis. Serv. ch. 588 (A.B. 26).

28   *See* Strauss v. Horton, 207 P.3d 48, 65 (Cal. 2009).

29   *See* 2001 Cal. Legis. Serv. ch. 893 (A.B. 25).

30   539 U.S. 558 (2003).

31   478 U.S. 186 (1986).

32   *See Lawrence,* 539 U.S. at 600-05 (Scalia, J., dissenting).

33   *See* Goodridge v. Department of Public Health, 798 N.E.2d 941 (Mass. 2003).

34   *See In re* Opinion of the Justices to the Senate, 802 N.E.2d 565 (Mass. 2004).

35   *See Goodridge,* 798 N.E.2d at 948, 953, 958 n.17, 959,

961 n.23, 962.

36   *See id.* at 969-70.

37   *See* 2003 Cal. Legis. Serv. ch. 421 (A.B. 205).

38   *See* 2003 N.J. Sess. Law Serv. ch. 246 (Assembly 3743).

39   *See* Lockyer v. City and County of San Francisco, 95 P.3d 459, 464-65 (Cal. 2004).

40   *See* Li v. State, 110 P.3d 91, 94-95 (Or. 2005).

41   *See* Hebel v. West, 803 N.Y.S.2d 242, 244 (2005).

42   *See* Li v. State, 110 P.3d 91 (Or. 2005); Lockyer v. City and County of San Francisco, 95 P.3d 459 (Cal. 2004).

43   *See* 2004 Me. Legis. Serv. ch. 672 (H.P. 1152).

44   *See* Kerrigan v. Commissioner of Public Health, 957 A.2d 407, 413 (Conn. 2008).

45   *See In re* Marriage Cases, 183 P.3d 384, 410 n.17 (Cal. 2008).

46   *See* Andersen v. King County, 138 P.3d 963 (Wash. 2006); Hernandez v. Robles, 855 N.E.2d 1 (N.Y. 2006).

47   *See* 2005 N.J. Sess. Law Serv. ch. 331 (Senate 2083).

48   *See* Lewis v. Harris, 908 A.2d 196 (N.J. 2006).

49   *See* 2006 N.J. Sess. Law ch. 103 (Assembly 3787).

50   *See* Conaway v. Deane, 932 A.2d 571 (Md. 2007).

51   *See* 2007 N.H. Laws 58:1.

52   *See* Lynne Marie Kohm, *Family and Juvenile Law*, 42 U. Rich. L. Rev. 417, 422 n.26 (2007).

53   *See* 2007 Wash. Legis. Serv. ch. 156 (S.S.B. 5336).

54   *See* 2007 Or. Laws ch. 99 (H.B. 2007).

55   *See* 2008 Wash. Legis. Serv. ch. 6 (S.S.H.B. 3104).

56   *See In re* Marriage Cases, 183 P.3d 384 (Cal. 2008).

57   *See* Strauss v. Horton, 207 P.3d 48 (Cal. 2009).

58   *See* Kerrigan v. Commissioner of Public Health, 957 A.2d 407 (Conn. 2008).

59   *See* Conn. Const. Art. 13, § 2.

60   *See* 2009 Conn. P.A. 09-13 (S.B. 899).

61   *See* 2008 Md. Laws ch. 590 (S.B. 566).

62   *See* 2009 N.H. Laws 59:1; 2009 Vt. Laws No. 3 (S. 115).

63   *See* Varnum v. Brien, 763 N.W.2d 862 (Iowa 2009).

64   *See* 2009 Wash. Legis. Serv. ch. 521 (E.S.S.S.B. 5688).

65   *See* 2009 Nevada Laws ch. 393 (S.B. 283).

66   *See* 2009 Colo. Legis. Serv. ch. 107 (HB 09-1260).

67   *See* 2009-10 Wis. Legis. Serv. Act 28 (2009 A.B. 75).

68   *See* 2009 D.C. Laws 18-110 (Act 18-248).

69   *See* Gill v. Office of Personnel Management, 699 F. Supp. 2d 374 (D. Mass. 2010); Massachusetts v. U.S. Department of Health & Human Services, 698 F. Supp. 2d 234 (D. Mass. 2010).

70   *See* Perry v. Schwarzenegger, 704 F. Supp. 2d 921 (N.D. Cal. 2010).

71   *See* 2011 Haw. Sess. Laws 1 (S.B. 232); 2010 Ill. Legis. Serv. P.A. 96-1513 (S.B. 1716).

72   *See* 78 Del. Laws ch. 22 (S.B. 30) (2011).

73   *See* Christiansen v. Christiansen, 253 P.3d 153 (Wyo. 2011).

74   *See* 2011 N.Y. Laws ch. 95 (A. 8354).

75   *See* 2011 R.I. Pub. Laws 11-198 (11-H 6103A).

76   *See* 2012 Md. Laws ch. 2 (H.B. 438); 2012 Wash. Legis. Serv. ch. 3 (S.S.B. 6239).

77   *See* Perry v. Brown, 671 F.3d 1052 (9th Cir. 2012).

78   *See* Massachusetts v. U.S. Department of Health and Human Services, 682 F.3d 1 (1st Cir. 2012).

79   *See* Windsor v. United States, 699 F.3d 169 (2d Cir. 2012).

80   *See* United States v. Windsor, 133 S. Ct. 786 (2012); Hollingsworth v. Perry, 133 S. Ct. 786 (2012)

81   *See* 2013 Colo. Legis. Serv. ch. 49 (S.B. 13-011).

82   *See* 79 Del. Laws ch. 19 (H.B. 75) (2013).

83   *See* 2013 Minn. Sess. Law Serv. ch. 74 (H.F. 1054).

84   *See* 2013 R.I. Sess. Laws ch. 13-4, 13-5 (13-H 5015B, 13-S 38A).

85   133 S. Ct. 2652 (2013).

86   133 S. Ct. 2675 (2013).

87   *See id.* at 2709-10 (Scalia, J., dissenting).

88   *See* Notice 2013-61, 2013-44 I.R.B. 432; Statement from Secretary of Homeland Security Janet Napolitano (July 1, 2013).

89   *See* POMS § GN 00210.000, *Windsor* Same-Sex

Marriage Claims.

90 *See* Commonwealth, Dep't of Health v. Hanes, 78 A.3d 676 (Pa. Cmwlth. 2013).

91 *See* Garden State Equality v. Dow, 2013 WL 5397372 (N.J. Super. Ct. Law Div. Sept. 27, 2013).

92 *See* Garden State Equality v. Dow, 2013 WL 5687193 (N.J. Oct. 18, 2013).

93 *See* Kate Zernike & Marc Santora, *As Gays Marry in New Jersey, Christie Yields*, N.Y. TIMES, Oct. 22, 2013, at A1.

94 *See* 2013 Haw. Laws 2nd Sp. Sess. Act 1 (S.B. 1).

95 *See* 2013 Ill. Legis. Serv. P.A. 98-597 (S.B. 10).

96 *See* Lee v. Orr, 2013 WL 6490577 (N.D. Ill. Dec. 10, 2013); Gray v. Orr, 2013 WL 6355918 (N.D. Ill. Dec. 5, 2013).

97 *See* Griego v. Oliver, 2013 WL 6670704 (N.M. Dec. 19, 2013).

98 *See id.*; Fernanda Santos & Heath Haussamen, *Marriage Licenses for Same-Sex Couples Force Issue to Fore in New Mexico*, N.Y. TIMES, Sept. 3, 2013, at A12.

99 *See* Obergefell v. Wymyslo, 2013 WL 6726688, at *1 & n.1 (S.D. Ohio Dec. 23, 2013); Kitchen v. Herbert, 2013 WL 6697874, at *7-8, 17, 22, 27-28 (D. Utah Dec. 20, 2013).

100 *See* Obergefell v. Wymyslo, 2013 WL 6726688 (S.D. Ohio Dec. 23, 2013).

101 *See* Kitchen v. Herbert, 2013 WL 6697874 (D. Utah Dec. 20, 2013).

102 *See* Herbert v. Kitchen, 2014 WL 30367 (2014).

103 The one slight exception is in New Hampshire, where the minimum age for marriage is 18, but which allows opposite-sex marriage (but not same-sex marriage) for males as young as 14 and females as young as 13 with parental consent. *See* N.H. Rev. Stat. §§ 457:4-6.

104 Same-sex marriages were halted in November, 2008 as a result of a constitutional amendment, and resumed in June, 2013 when litigation over the amendment's constitutionality was finalized.

105 The law itself was enacted by the legislature in 2013, but it did not go into effect until June 1, 2014. However, pursuant to decisions by a federal district court, couples in which one partner has a life-threatening illness can marry prior to that date. *See* Lee v. Orr, 2013 WL 6490577 (N.D. Ill. Dec. 10, 2013); Gray v. Orr, 2013 WL 6355918 (N.D. Ill. Dec. 5, 2013).

106 The law itself was enacted by the legislature in 2012, but it did not go into effect until 2013.

107 In 2008, the Maryland Legislature created a statewide of definition of "domestic partner," and granted such persons a limited number of rights, but there was no formal registry or method of creating or dissolving such relationships.

108 The court decision itself was issued in 2003, but the Massachusetts Supreme Judicial Court stayed its ruling until early 2004.

109 The law itself was enacted by the legislature in 2009, but it did not go into effect until 2010.

110 This is the fee for obtaining a license; an additional fee is typically charged to obtain a copy of the marriage certificate.

111 Can marry at a younger age with parental and judicial consent (or, in rare instances, judicial consent alone). *See* Cal. Fam. Code §§ 301-304.

112 Personal appearance requirement can be waived for members of the armed forces or for those who are physically unable to appear in person, such as those who are incarcerated or hospitalized. *See* Cal. Fam. Code §§ 354(e), 359(a), 420(b), 426.

113 Can marry at age 16 with parental consent (or, in rare instances, judicial consent alone); can marry below age 16 with parental and judicial consent (or, in rare instances, judicial consent alone). *See* Conn. Gen. Stat. §§ 46b-20a, 46b-30.

114 The fee is $100 for non-residents.

115 Can marry at a younger age with judicial consent. *See* Del. Code Ann. tit. 13, § 123.

116 Personal appearance requirement can be waived for a party too ill to appear in person. *See* Del. Code Ann. tit. 13, § 120.

117 Can marry at age 16 with parental consent, or at age 15 with parental and judicial consent. *See* Haw. Rev. Stat. §§ 572-1, 571-2.

118 Not available to residents of states where such a marriage is deemed void. *See* 750 Ill. Comp. Stat. 5/217.

119 Can marry at age 16 with parental or judicial consent.

See 750 Ill. Comp. Stat. 5/203, 5/208.

120 Can marry at age 16 with parental and judicial consent (or, in rare instances, judicial consent alone). *See* Iowa Code § 595.2.

121 Can be waived with judicial order. *See* Iowa Code § 595.4.

122 Can marry at age 16 or 17 with parental consent, and below age 16 with parental and judicial consent. *See* Me. Rev. Stat. tit. 19-A, § 652(7), (8).

123 Can marry at age 16 or 17 with parental consent or if a female party to the marriage is pregnant or has given birth. Can marry at age 15 if a female party to the marriage is pregnant or has given birth and a parent consents. *See* Md. Code, Fam. Law § 2-301.

124 The waiting period can be waived by judicial order. *See* Md. Code, Fam. Law § 2-405(d)(2).

125 Can marry at a younger age with parental and judicial consent (or, in rare instances, judicial consent alone). *See* Mass. Gen. Laws ch. 207, §§ 7, 25.

126 Can be waived with judicial order. *See* Mass. Gen. Laws ch. 207, §§ 19, 28, 30.

127 If a party is too ill to appear in person, the oath can be taken on their behalf by a parent, guardian, or the other party if a physician's affidavit is provided. *See* Mass. Gen. Laws ch. 207, § 20.

128 The fee is reduced to $40 for those who have completed 12 hours of premarital counseling. *See* Minn. Stat. § 517.08.

129 Can marry at age 16 with parental and judicial consent. *See* Minn. Stat. § 517.02

130 Can be waived by judicial order. *See* Minn. Stat. § 517.08.

131 Not available to residents of states where such a marriage is deemed void. *See* N.H. Rev. Stat. Ann. § 457:44.

132 For opposite-sex couples, males as young as 14 and females as young as 13 can marry with parental and judicial consent if at least one of them is a New Hampshire resident. *See* N.H. Rev. Stat. Ann. §§ 457:4, 457:5, 457:6.

133 Personal appearance requirement can be waived for members of the armed forces. *See* N.H. Rev. Stat. Ann. § 5-C:42, V.

134 Can marry at age 16 or 17 with parental consent, and below age 16 with parental and judicial consent. *See* N.J. Stat. Ann. § 37:1-6.

135 Can be waived with judicial order. *See* N.J. Stat. Ann. § 37:1-4.

136 Personal appearance requirement can be waived for one partner if they are a member of the armed forces. *See* N.J. Stat. Ann. §§ 37:1-8, 37:1-17.3.

137 Can marry at age 16 or 17 with parental consent, and below age 16 with parental and judicial consent. *See* N.M. Stat. Ann. § 40-1-6.

138 Personal appearance requirement can be waived by judicial order. *See* N.M. Stat. Ann. § 40-1-10.

139 The fee is $35 in New York City and $40 in the rest of the state.

140 Sickle cell anemia test required for those "not of the Caucasian, Indian or Oriental race." N.Y. Dom. Rel. Law § 13-aa.

141 Can marry at age 16 or 17 with parental consent, and at age 14 or 15 with parental and judicial consent. *See* N.Y. Dom. Rel. Law §§ 15, 15-a.

142 Waiting period may be waived with judicial approval. *See* N.Y. Dom. Rel. Law § 13-b.

143 If one of the parties is a member of the armed services, the license's validity can be extended to 180 days. *See* N.Y. Exec. Law § 354-d.

144 Females can marry at age 16 with parental consent. Males younger than 18 and females younger than 16 can marry with parental and judicial consent. *See* R.I. Gen. Laws § 15-2-11.

145 Can marry at age 16 or 17 with parental consent, and at age 15 with parental and judicial consent. *See* Utah Code Ann. § 30-1-9.

146 Can marry at age 16 with parental consent. *See* Vt. Stat. Ann. tit. 1, § 173; *id.* tit. 18, § 5142.

147 Can marry at age 17 with parental consent, and below age 17 with judicial consent. *See* Rev. Code Wash. Ann. §§ 26.040.010, 26.040.210(1).

148 Can marry at age 16 with parental consent. *See* D.C. Code §§ 46-403, 46-411.

149 Waiting period can be waived with judicial order. *See* D.C. Code § 46-418.

150 Colorado's civil union program was preceded by a designated beneficiary program, which still exists.

151 The only exception is that employers need not offer health care benefits to the domestic partners of employees. *See* Nev. Rev. Stat. § 122A.210.

152 Although enacted in 2007, the domestic partnership program in Oregon did not go into effect until 2008.

153 Colorado permits couples to perform their own ceremony by means of self-certification.

154 *See* Colo. Rev. Stat. § 14-15-115.

155 *See* Or. Rev. Stat. Ann. § 106.325(4).

156 *See* Cal. Fam. Code § 2320(b).

157 *See* Del. Code Ann. tit. 13, § 1504.

158 *See* D.C. Code § 16-902.

159 *See* Haw. Rev. Stat. § 580-1.

160 *See* 750 Ill. Comp. Stat. 5/220.

161 *See* Minn. Stat. § 518.07.

162 *See* Vt. Stat. Ann. tit. 15, § 592(b).

163 *See* Atwood v. Riviotta, 2013 WL 2150021 (Ariz. App. Div 1 2013); Surnamer v. Ellstrom, 2012 WL 2864412 (Ariz. App. Div 1 2012).

164 *See* Cal Fam. Code §§ 299.2, 308. California's complex scheme for recognizing out-of-state unions was enacted in the wake of Proposition 8 and will probably be amended to recognize out-of-state unions as marriages.

165 *See* Colo. Rev. Stat. § 14-15-116.

166 *See* Conn. Gen. Stat. Ann. § 46b-28a.

167 *See* Del. Code Ann. tit. 13, § 101(e); Anonymous v. Anonymous, 85 A. 2d 706, 715 (Del. Super. Ct. New Castle Co. 1951).

168 *See* Haw. Rev. Stat. §§ 572-3, 572B-10.

169 *See* 750 Ill. Comp. Stat. 75/60.

170 *See In re* Reed's Marriage, 226 N.W.2d 795, 796 (Iowa 1975).

171 *See* Me. Rev. Stat. Ann. tit. 19-A, § 650-B.

172 *See* Port v. Cowan, 44 A.3d 970 (Md. 2012).

173 *See* Hunter v. Rose, 975 N.E.2d 857 (Mass. 2012); Elia-Warnken v. Elia, 972 N.E.2d 17 (Mass. 2012).

174 *See* Johnson v. Johnson, 8 N.W. 2d 620, 622-23 (Minn. 1943).

175 *See* Nev. Rev. Stat. Ann. 122A.500.

176 *See* N.H. Rev. Stat. §§ 457:3, 457:45.

177 *See* N.J. Stat. Ann. §§ 26:8A-6(c), 37:1-34; Opinion of the New Jersey Attorney General 3-2007, 2007 WL 749807 (Feb. 16, 2007); www.state.nj.us/health/vital/faq.shtml#ssm (last visited Dec. 28, 2013).

178 *See* N.M. Stat. Ann. § 40-1-4; Griego v. Oliver, 2013 WL 6670704 (N.M. Dec. 19, 2013).

179 *See* Dickerson v. Thompson, 897 N.Y.S.2d 298 (N.Y. App. Div. 2010); Lewis v. NYS Dep't of Civil Service, 872 N.Y.S.2d 578 (N.Y. App. Div. 2009).

180 *See* Obergefell v. Wymyslo, 2013 WL 6726688 (S.D. Ohio Dec. 23, 2013).

181 *See* Opinion of the Oregon Attorney General (Oct. 16, 2013).

182 *See* R.I. Gen. Laws § 15-1-8; *Ex parte Chace*, 58 A. 978 (R.I. 1904).

183 *See* Kitchen v. Herbert, 2013 WL 6697874 (D. Utah Dec. 20, 2013).

184 *See* Wheelock v. Wheelock, 154 A. 665 (Vt. 1931).

185 *See* Rev. Code Wash. Ann. §§ 26.04, 26.04.020.

186 *See* D.C. Code § 46-405.1.

187 *See* Wisc. Const. Art. 13, § 13.

188 *See* Wyo. Stat. § 20-1-111; Christiansen v. Christiansen, 253 P.3d 153 (Wyo. 2011).

189 There is some uncertainty as to whether Oklahoma's amendment bans recognition of just same-sex marriages or if it also bans recognition of other types of relationships. On the one hand, after defining marriage as the union of one man and one woman, the amendment provides that "[n]either this Constitution nor any other provision of law shall be construed to require that marital status or the legal incidents thereof be conferred upon unmarried couples or groups," Okla. Const. art. 2, § 35—language that arguably encompasses recognition of civil unions or domestic partnerships. On the other hand, a federal district court considering a challenge to the constitutionality of the Oklahoma amendment interpreted it as banning only recognition of marriage, not civil unions. *See* Bishop v. Oklahoma *ex. rel.* Edmondson, 447 F. Supp. 2d 1239, 1256 (N.D. Okla. 2006), *rev'd on other grounds*, 333 Fed. Appx. 361 (10th Cir. 2009).

190 Connecticut requires either a supermajority vote or a majority vote in two successive sessions.

191 In Delaware, voters play no role in the constitutional amendment process.

192 Illinois permits citizen-initiated constitutional amendments for amending some parts of the constitution, but not those dealing with individual rights.

193 It must receive support from 3/5 of those voting on the question or a majority of those voting in that election for any office.

194 Massachusetts permits *indirect* citizen-initiated amendments, in that the amendment can be initiated by citizens, but requires the approval of 25 percent of a joint session of the legislature before placement on the ballot.

195 It must receive support from a majority of those voting in that election for any office.

196 New Jersey requires either a supermajority vote or a majority vote in two successive sessions.

197 While a 2/3 vote is required in the Senate, only a majority of the house is required.

198 *See* Jesse McKinley & Laurie Goodstein, *Bans in 3 States on Gay Marriage*, N.Y. TIMES, Nov. 6, 2008, at A1.

About the Authors

PETER NICOLAS is the Jeffrey & Susan Brotman Professor of Law and Adjunct Professor of Gender, Women & Sexuality Studies at the University of Washington. He specializes in sexual orientation law and constitutional law, and is the author of a textbook and numerous journal articles on gay rights and same-sex marriage. He is the winner of the prestigious Dukeminier Award, awarded annually to the authors of the best sexual orientation and gender identity law journal articles published each year.

MIKE STRONG is based in Seattle, Washington. He is a specialist in Geographic Information Systems (GIS), and has worked for local governments and government agencies throughout the Puget Sound area and Washington State.

CPSIA information can be obtained
at www.ICGtesting.com
Printed in the USA
LVIC06n1520071214
417645LV00014B/62